MOTHER'S LITTLE ALIBI

LYDIA CONSTANTINE

CONTENTS

COPYRIGHT

Print Paperback ISBN-13: 979-8-9911658-0-8
Print Hardcover ISBN-13: 979-8-9911658-1-5
Printed 2024 Sikeston, MO, USA
Library of Congress Control Number: 2024915418

PREFACE

Everyone thought Allen was odd and a "momma's boy." He was 48 years old and still living at home. It was such a small house that you had to know where it was to find it. The giant horse-weeds were taller than the house, which had not been painted since his father died thirty years ago. Only tracks in the driveway made by the daily trip in and out gave you a clue someone lived there. That trip took them to a local restaurant called The Diner, where they sat by themselves daily and ordered one meal, which they shared. All the locals knew them but never had any encouragement offered that might make them want to befriend them. My mother and I ate lunch there daily but we also were guilty of not paying attention to this strange couple.

One day in early autumn, things started to change. The humidity was still as high as it had been in the summer and everyone was still dressed in summer clothes. Allen brought Momma into The Diner dressed in a cotton dress that was obviously too large for her. Momma continued to get thinner each day, but Allen stayed the same. Everyone speculated that the only meal of the day that Momma received was at The Diner. Allen always ordered the "Special of the Day" which was composed of a meat, two vegetables, a slice of white bread and dessert. He shared this with Momma, but she ate very little and seemed to grow quieter day by day.

Around Labor Day, Allen began to come in by himself, leaving Momma in the car parked under a shade tree. Allen ate the whole meal and did not take anything out to Momma. Everyone was concerned but no one was bothered enough to get involved. Some weeks later, Allen pulled into the gas station a few blocks down from The Diner for fuel. The attendant who was washing the windshield noticed an odor, then saw that Momma was slumped over in the car. He asked Allen about Momma, which agitated Allen. He jumped into the car without paying the attendant for the gas and drove quickly away. The attendant called the local police.

The police stopped the car before he made it to the driveway. Upon calling the coroner, they discovered that Momma had been dead for at least two weeks. When Allen was asked what had happened, he said, "She went to sleep so I figured she would wake up when she got hungry." Allen was sent to a mental institution and the county bulldozed the house, as it was too filthy to renovate and sell. The county also buried Momma in a pine box since there was not enough money to take care of her.

This sad death made the headlines of our local newspaper, a weekly called the *Weston Standard*. The *Weston* was a small-town publication with a lot of social information about birthdays, weddings, obituaries and births. Sports often made the front page as sporting events were always covered in all the surrounding small towns. An elderly lady wrote a gossip page called "Hometown Happenings" that told you of parties and who attended. To have yourself on the front page for any reason was something to be proud of. To land something really newsworthy like Allen's Mom was exceptional.

That death replaced the news item headlined, "Local Dog Rides on Top of Owner's Pickup Truck," which was scheduled to run that weekend. This upset and disappointed Billy Bob Malone, proud owner of Bubba's Baby (a hound dog - golden retriever mix) that was the result of a fence-climbing golden retriever named Sir Galahad. This was a strange-looking dog, but was the love of Billy Bob's life. He was so proud of this dog, that on Sunday mornings, Bubba's Baby ate pancakes sitting at the table with the family. He had already told all his friends to be sure to get the Sunday paper so they could see him and Bubba's Baby. Now it was not to be.

I was 13 when this happened, and I had just started to live a "normal life" two years before. It seems that until I was 11, my family had been the topic of conversation and gossip, frequently making the headlines or the telephone party lines. I'm also going to tell you about life in a small town, and the neighbors that grew up what was considered "normal." Those eleven prior years is what this story is about. But first you need to know the history of my family and how we arrived at this point.

CHAPTER 1

THE CLAYS

My name is Lydia and this is a true story. I entered the world a breach birth at home in May, 1943 to a beautiful but vain mother named Ava who was the baby of her family. Her father, Noble Clay, was very wealthy due to an inheritance from his mother, Callista Ryan. Callista died of consumption, better known as tuberculosis, at the age of 21. Noble was 10 months old at the time she died and was raised by his father until he remarried several years later.

Noble's mother, Callista, had been very well educated as her brothers were lawyers and she had also begun to study law. Her family were prominent farmers in Indiana who had moved from the East Coast with a large group of other adventurers. They had purchased good farmland and had prospered in this uncharted part of the country. She had been given a large amount of money, as a wedding gift, when she married Noble's father, John Clay. She married in 1879, when she was 19 and John was 21. Noble's father never touched Callista's money as he had a very successful business that he had owned for a few years prior to the marriage. He was very frugal. He saved what profit he made for additional land purchases. They also invested Callista's money.

John's business was "threshing" crops across Texas, Kansas, Oklahoma and Missouri. This modern technology replaced crop harvesting by hand. The sheaves of grain would be carried to the thresher by the farmworkers. John owned a large Case-brand steam engine, and as the wheels rotated, sheaves of grain were forced against the wheel, and the ribs knocked the grain from the heads. The grain would then be bagged by the crew, and the stalks would be bundled into straw for animal bedding and other purposes. Wheat was the majority of the grain harvested, followed by oats, barley, buckwheat and rye.

Until the invention of steam engines, threshing machines were powered by draft animals, hitched to horsepower that transferred their motion to the machine. Noble's father's modern steam tractor was faster and more efficient getting the crops out than the horse-powered machines. He would travel to one state, work several farms starting in the south, then move his equipment north following the maturity of the crops. This alleviated some of the worry that the farmers had about getting their crops out. This machine would harvest quickly between weather events. The moment the crop was finished, John would move to the next farm and/or state to pursue another harvest.

He used the train system to transport the heavy tractors and other equipment from place to place. He had a crew of men and women who traveled with him on the train to do the manual work. The crew consisted of mechanics to keep the machine running, women to do the cooking and laundry, and other male employees to do all the things necessary to assemble and take apart the equipment for transfer. The employees also managed the harvesting, seeing that everything fell in line perfectly from harvest to delivery. Much of his clientele was repeat business. It was a very profitable business.

What a happy year 1883 was for the young couple! Callista became pregnant in what was her fourth year of marriage. She and John were very excited about their new baby. Everything seemed to be good for them until Callista began to cough up blood in the beginning of her seventh month of pregnancy. There was no cure for what they called consumption. The only thing that seemed to help prolong the life of a patient was to move from a high-humidity area to a dry-humidity state. They chose Texas and moved their home to a small area called Denton, next to Dallas. They used some of their money to purchase a farm in hopes they could keep her alive. Callista gave birth to Noble and enjoyed the role of motherhood for ten months. When Noble turned 8 months old, her health began to fail dramatically. She was having difficulty breathing, losing weight and becoming very fatigued. They could see that the climate was not helping her, as she was beginning to cough up blood again. They decided to bring her home to Indiana to die. By the time Noble was 10 months old, his mother was gone.

Noble's mother's untimely death caused hardship for John's business. His heart was broken because of losing his young wife and he had to let his business go the last few months. He stayed in Indiana until she was buried. Organizing his crew and getting started again was difficult. His heart was not in it. Finding someone to take care of Noble was a problem as he had promised Callista he would not leave his only son behind. Neither John's parents nor her parents, the Ryans, were young enough to take care of the child while he was gone for such a long time, during harvest.

John thought about hiring a young woman to travel with the crew. He put an ad in the paper for this position, but the women who applied were either not of very good character, too old, too young or not interested in being gone that long. Many would not consider the job as it was not acceptable to have a single woman traveling with the crew. The women presently traveling with him were hired to cook, wash laundry and were wives of the crew. Often, they would have their own children with them. Sometimes the women would volunteer to help, but Noble was not as old as the other children and required more care.

When they were in Indian territory, Noble was sometimes babysat by Indian women during the day and stayed with his father at night. This was much better as the women they found for this job were older and could give him more attention. The same Indian women babysat each year. As the years went by, Noble picked up on some of the Indian languages of his sitters in Oklahoma and Kansas. He was very fond of his Indian friends, the Shawnee and the Pawnee, and they enjoyed him. They shared Indian stories that he loved to share with his family when he was a grown man. He had been given arrow heads and other items from the Indian culture that he always treasured his whole life.

Finally, his father remarried and Noble had a real mother to take care of him. He still traveled with his father's business after he finished high school. At the age of 21, he ceased to go, as by that time he had inherited his mother's and grandparents' money. His father also had a new family, but by that time they were considerably younger than Noble.

Noble was tall, with beautiful blond hair and crystal-blue eyes. He had a wit and charm that was captivating. At the age of 21, he fell in love with a local farmer's daughter, age 14, named Clarissa Clay. Clarissa was the oldest child in her family. Her father was a small farmer barely making a living supporting eight children. Clarissa spent her days helping her mother with all the household chores. She helped take care of her siblings. She also learned to embroider and quilt. Quilting seemed to be an artistic talent for her, as she soon developed her own patterns for quilting, instead of using the traditional ones that all her sisters were using. She had been taken out of school after the second grade, but had learned to read and write. She was encouraged by her parents and her brothers to learn math and further expand her knowledge of reading at home. Her brothers attended school, so they often helped her study their textbooks.

Boys were always educated in most families as they needed to know about business. Women were educated at home to be a wife and mother. Clarissa was a brunette with deep brown eyes and a natural beauty that required no make-up. She was very impressed with this handsome young man she had met at a wedding. He was in love with her from the very first day he met her. He started courting her with her parents' permission. Noble was well educated as a farmer but had not learned to manage money. He had a buggy, wore expensive clothes and was well groomed. Her parents were impressed with the personable young man. He soon talked her parents into letting her marry him. They knew they were very much in love and that he had the money to support her, so they agreed. The marriage took place in 1905. Clarissa had no jewelry, so Noble's half sister, Tess, loaned her gold watch to Clarissa to wear for the wedding picture With Clarissa leaving home, there would be more money to educate the boys. This marriage proposal would also mean a good home for Clarissa.

After a few years of moving around, as his young family grew, Noble purchased 440 acres and he and Clarissa moved into a beautiful eight-room home. Noble had built the home with his mother's money. He hired a cook-maid to take care of the house and family. He raised cattle and hogs and crops. In addition to farming, he was a livestock dealer and would ship carloads of cattle or hogs to the city. The couple produced seven children, four boys and three girls in this home. Alvin was the oldest son, with Seth only nineteen months younger. Two other boys, Matthew and John, were born later, followed by Ann, Adeline and Ava who was the baby. Only one child did not survive past childhood.

CHAPTER 2

BIRTH OF MY MOTHER, AVA

Ava was born in November 1918, on the day World War I ended. The bells were ringing in all the churches and the train whistles were blowing in the small town celebrating this glorious occasion. Clarissa was beginning to show signs of labor and was suffering from the flu. Noble had gone to town to get the doctor to come help with the delivery, medical supplies for Clarissa as well as the children who had the flu, and groceries. Noble had left Ann who was only 5, to attend to the needs of the whole family while he went for the doctor. Ann was playing in the yard when she heard the noises. There were guns being fired and people yelling and singing! She ran inside to ask her mother what it was she heard. Her mother did not know for sure. Just then a neighbor poked his head in the door and yelled that the War was over and peace had been declared!

There was no celebration of the Declaration of Peace in the Clay household, while Ava was being born. Noble had returned from town with bad news. The doctor could not come to deliver the baby. The doctor was inundated with multiple patients he was trying to save from the Spanish Flu. The doctor had run out of all medication for the flu and was unable to get any more to help

Noble's family. Fifty million people in the world died of the flu and it did not end until 1920. The victims died within hours or days of developing symptoms. Their skin would turn blue and their lungs would fill with fluid that caused them to suffocate. There were people that recovered from the flu who must have had some measure of immunity, and some never got the disease at all.

There was no help from the maid who took care of the Clay family. She had gone home to help with her own family illnesses and was not expected to come back until the pandemic was over.

Clarissa had a severe case of the flu and by this time she was in the last minutes of her labor. The only members of the family that had escaped the flu, were Ava's 5-year-old sister, Ann, and her father. It was up to Noble and Ann to deliver the baby, and they rehearsed what the doctor had told them to do. Fortunately, there were no complications, because once her labor started there was no turning back.

The next crucial problem started with how to feed the baby, as Clarissa could not nurse Ava since she had an active case of the flu. They had no other source for Ava's survival other than cow's milk. The doctor had told Noble not to give her cow's milk as it was too rich and she would develop severe diarrhea. Instead, he told him to take a clean handkerchief or a thin cotton glove and make a "sugar tit." You made the "tit" by placing wet sugar or honey in the center of the handkerchief or the fingertips of the glove. A small hole was then punched in the end with a large needle. Then the baby could suck the contents out and it could be refilled. A small amount of water was given after each feeding. Ava would need to be fed every two hours until Clarissa's milk "came in," and she was well enough to nurse.

Noble and Ann took turns using this method to feed her for several days. In between, they had to feed the four boys and their mother, who were all sick, and tend to their needs. The youngest child, a sister named Adeline, was only 2 and not faring as well as the boys. It was difficult to get her to eat or drink liquids. She required a lot more attention from Noble, as Ann was too little to hold and console her. She cried a lot which further complicated her breathing. Noble would rock her and sing lullabies trying to get her calmed down. The boys would be asking for water and food, and Ann would have to run those items to them while Noble was occupied with the toddler.

In any spare time, Ann had been told to sit on the porch and read or play with her doll. Just stay away from the illness inside as much as possible. While sitting on the porch every day, Ann watched people in horse-drawn carriages and buckboards carrying the bodies of the dead to the cemetery which was just past their home. Oftentimes the bodies would be stacked in the buckboards without any family members able to attend a service for them. Few of these bodies were dressed for a regular burial. Some were in their nightgowns or their underwear. They all had one thing in common—they were blue! Then taken to the grave-yard, a minister would say a few words over the bodies. If they had a family plot, they would be buried there. If not, they would be buried in the dirt along the edge of the cemetery with a stick marker with their name on it. Few had coffins, as the funeral home was swamped with bodies, and the funeral home owners were often sick themselves. Many times, parents were walking or on horseback carrying dead babies and small children and a shovel to bury their child or children, themselves. Any Christian burials would have to be attended by a relative with a Bible, or if you were lucky, a preacher who did not have the flu.

No one knew at the time that Adeline would be one of the flu casualties. Adeline died a week after Ava's birth. She just didn't wake up in the morning. It was hard for Noble to tell Clarissa. He knew she would be worried about Ava, too. The only good news was the boys were beginning to improve. Noble wrapped Adeline in a white blanket to be taken to the cemetery. Ann and Alvin were the only children well enough to go. Clarissa insisted on riding to the cemetery in a buckboard that carried the small coffin Noble had made. Noble could not talk her out of it, so he helped her onto the buckboard seat and handed her Ava. Clarissa was recovering but was very weak from the flu and the childbirth. She was determined to be with her child until the last, so she handed Ava to Alvin. Ann and Alvin climbed onto the buckboard next to the coffin. Clarissa asked to hold Adeline all the way to the cemetery. She bent over her and wept unconsolably. Ann carried the family Bible so that Noble might read the scriptures that he thought were appropriate for such a young child. Clarissa had never lost a child before and was sobbing. She prayed out loud for the soul of this daughter, whom she could not hold and comfort in her final hours.

When they arrived at the cemetery, Noble took Adeline from her mother's arms and hugged the little body as the tears he had been holding back streamed down his face. He then placed her in the coffin and he helped Clarissa to the ground. Alvin and Ann started crying, too, as they were so shocked to see their father cry. Alvin dug the grave and they said the appropriate words and good-byes. As sad as it was, not many families were as fortunate as the Clays to only lose one child. Immunity was the only thing that could help you, and this family must have been exceptionally healthy.

Once Clarissa was able to nurse Ava, she began to thrive. From there forward, Ava grew up until the age of 5 with a maid, beautiful clothes and the best of everything. Her older siblings were all being educated and everything seemed good in their lives.

CHAPTER 3

MOLLY MOVES IN

When Ava was 3, a 31-year-old cousin of Clarissa's, named Molly, became homeless after losing her husband and parents. She had auburn hair and green eyes. She was very striking. She was a schoolteacher in need of a home to stay in temporarily. Molly's stay developed into a long-term visit. Perhaps having a maid-cook so she did not have any domestic duties, appealed to her. Two years later, she was still there.

When Molly moved in, she had plenty of men who were interested in dating her. She dated several local men until the second year, when she appeared to have lost interest in dating. She was always dressed in the latest fashions, and since she had to pay no rent, she could spend her money she made teaching, as she pleased. Most of the money went toward jewelry, purses, hats and shoes to accessorize herself to look her very best. Noble took her to and from school every day so she did not have to walk. He had built their home on a farm so he had hired plenty of help to work the acreage. He had become a "gentleman farmer," someone who merely rides around looking at the farm and gives directions to the help. Molly liked to ride around with him, looking at the crops. They began taking a detour on the ride home from school for this purpose. Clarissa was naïve and trusting about this daily event. Later, looking back, the whole family realized Molly's intent. Afterward, they also questioned if all her wardrobe had been paid for by her or if some of her attire was gifted by Noble.

In the spring of Ava's 5th year and her mother's seventeenth year of marriage, her father took what cash he had left in the bank and ran off to Texas with cousin Molly. Clarissa was shocked as she had no idea Noble had been having an affair with Molly. More importantly, the family did not know that Noble had squandered the rest of his inheritance on worthless farmland and oil wells in Texas. Over the past two years, he had mortgaged the farm, house, and everything in it to sustain the lifestyle that they had been living. The whole family was shocked and hurt to lose their father, but there were worse things to come.

A month after he left, the bank came calling, and Clarissa and her children were evicted. The first they knew about the eviction came early in the morning when they heard the animals outside making a lot of noise. When they looked out, they saw men running around on horses trying to round up the cattle. They had placed the other horses in a corral together. Noble's prized horse was among them. Other men were on foot, gathering up the chickens and putting them in a coop. The pigs were being loaded onto a buckboard. Clarissa ran into the yard yelling at the men, with her two oldest sons, Alvin and Seth behind her. She thought the men were thieves, so the boys were carrying rifles. One man, dressed in a business suit, stepped forward and handed Clarissa the eviction notice. She read it and told the boys to put down the guns, and the three of them went back to the house. Everyone was up by this time and dressed, except for Ava who was still in her nightgown.

Ann was 10 at the time, and she later said a large group of men were going through the house carrying out all the furniture. The first thing they took was a beautiful organ that had been a wedding present to Noble and Clarissa from his grandparents in

Indiana. All the children had been taught to play the organ including Ava, who cried as they carried it out. Ann tried consoling Ava by giving her doll to her to hold.

Clarissa went to the bedroom, locked the door, opened a small velvet box and took out a gold watch on a chain that she had worn on her wedding day. It had been loaned to her by her stepsister-in-law. She had since given it to Clarissa as a birthday gift. She also managed to get a gold locket on a chain that Noble had engraved with her initial, and that held a picture of Noble and her inside. Noble had a beautiful gold bracelet that had belonged to his mother, Callista, that he had given to Clarissa on their wedding day. She stuffed the three gold items between her breasts. She was anxious to have something she could sell for food if she had to do that. The gold was the only thing left that she could think of that might be of value to help her family survive.

The bank owner felt so sorry for Clarissa that they let them have some of their clothes, some quilts, a buckboard, a cow, two old horses and a sewing machine. The bank people said they had to load their family and possessions and be out of there by the next morning. They sat down to discuss what to do. Once the tears had ceased to flow, they discussed their options.

They ate what food that was left that was perishable and packed any food that could be eaten by cooking on a campfire. The bank had taken the boys' guns so there was no way to hunt for food, much less any streams to fish. It was decided that the two oldest boys, Alvin, who was 16, and Seth, 15, would ride the horses to Clarissa's father's home which was forty-nine miles away. The boys had never been away from home farther than a few miles. This troubled Clarissa as she felt she should be the one to stabilize the family. She worried that something might happen to the boys and, if so, she would never forgive herself. The bank had left the bridles, but had taken the saddles so they had to ride bareback. They did not know how to get there, so Clarissa wrote directions and told them to ask at the first homestead they came to for help if they were lost.

Once the boys arrived, they would tell their grandfather their dilemma and ask if there was any place the family could move near them. Whether or not the grandparents would have a place, the boys would return as soon as possible to let the family know the answer. She packed food for them and they left that afternoon. The whole family cried and the boys tried to act as if nothing was wrong. They said later they were very apprehensive about this adult responsibility that had been given them, but knew the family was dependent on them. They went as far as they could go in the daylight. They agreed that they would take turns keeping watch that night. But when they found a place for the horses to graze and get water, they both were so exhausted that neither one could stay awake. Wrapped in one of their mother's beautiful quilts, they slept peacefully.

The next morning, the younger children helped pack the wagon so that they would be able to leave as soon as the boys returned. They were prepared to stay in the yard until their family came back. When the bank people returned that morning to lock the doors to the house, they asked the family where they were going to go. When Clarissa told them they were waiting for their sons to return, they explained that they could not stay on this property that was no longer theirs. Once everything was locked up, they were asked to vacate.

Their neighbors had seen the bank car coming down the road, and like every small community, all of them knew what was happening. The neighbors followed the car and when they heard the dilemma, one offered a shed for shelter until their family returned for them. Another offered food. One farmer brought his horses to move the buckboard full of their remaining possessions off the farm as the boys were riding the horses that normally pulled the wagon. The family attended church regularly and were being offered full support from the members standing in the yard. Clarissa was reluctant to leave and move to the shed for fear they could not be found when her sons returned. The neighbors suggested they leave a note on the locked gate to tell them where they had gone. The bank agreed to let them do so.

We never knew how the news got to the boys' grandfather before they arrived. Possibly someone had been kind enough to pay for a telegram to be sent. The boys camped out two nights on the road. After the second night, they woke early and had ridden a few miles when they came upon their grandfather and one of their uncles. They both were on horseback and were carrying food and water. The boys were relieved to see them! They all quickly dismounted and there was hugging and a few tears. Then they all remounted and immediately started back to help their distressed family.

The family returned to the boys' homestead and prepared to help the rest of the family make the trip. Having no other place to go, they moved their family forty-nine miles to her father's farm. He had a four-room farmhouse that had previously been occupied by a sharecropper's family. He was hopeful it could be renovated enough to offer them shelter. They camped out on the way to their new home. With the buckboard loaded with the sewing machine and what few things they were allowed to keep, they started toward their new home. Because of the cow and the older children having to walk, the trip took three days. Although her father had brought food, those families the boys had come in contact with on the way to their grandparents', were kind enough to feed them again. Most of these families that helped had already heard the plight of this family from the boys' trip.

When they arrived at the house, they took care of the livestock and unloaded what few belongings they had left. They looked at what was to be their home and Clarissa finally broke down and cried. The smaller children cried with her. She said that this was the last tears she would shed. She was not crying because of the material things they had lost. She was crying in relief, because of all the stress that had happened the last few days and for her disappointment in Noble who she had loved for the past eighteen years.

This move affected Ava dramatically, but not any more than her older sister, Ann. Aunt Ann told me once that she had never worn anything but expensive store-bought clothes. By the time school started the next year, she had already outgrown them. They had no money for new ones so her mother used the sacks that flour came in to make her underwear. It was a thin cotton material with a floral print and she was devastated when all the girls at school made fun of her. She soon adapted to this way of life but Ava never did, and never forgave her father for deserting them and leaving them so destitute. Ava was the baby and had been spoiled by her father. His desertion broke her heart.

Clarissa knew she had to find some way to support her children in order to pay the tuition for school and the bus ride there. Although her father was generous, he was not a wealthy man. The boys handed down clothes, except for the oldest, who had to have new ones as he had outgrown his. This was another concern. She started doing other people's laundry. For additional income she rented out one of the rooms in the house. This meant the four boys would have to stay in one room and she and the girls would sleep in the living room area on a sofa and a pallet made from a quilt on the floor.

Their first renter was a young male schoolteacher for whom Clarissa provided meals and a stall for his mule that was his transportation. The only thing they found unpleasant about this arrangement was, during the winter, the renter was so fearful of being exposed to germs that he would wear an asphidity bag around his neck day and night. The bag was made of muslin and purchased from a pharmacy that stuffed it with various pungent herbs. They claimed it warded off diseases and evil spirits. It had such a strong smell that you could not stand to be near the person wearing it. Perhaps it was the social distancing caused by the odor that protected the individual, and not the medicinal ingredients. Also, his sense of smell must have died to endure the bag so close to his nose.

Clarissa was determined that all of her children would have an education so they might never experience how hard it was to not have one. All of her children eventually attended college, except for one. Her father helped her to buy shoes for those who had outgrown theirs. The boys had three pairs of overalls, and three shirts made from flour sacks and other materials that people had donated to them. They had three changes of underwear, socks and one pair of shoes. The girls had three dresses that their mother had made, as well as three pairs of flour-sack panties and undershirts. Every child had to wash their own clothes daily on a rub board in a black kettle filled with hot water and lye soap, that sat on a fire in the yard. After rinsing, they were hung to dry on the line, and if the weather was bad, put on the foot of the iron beds to dry. How this family existed through these hard times, with no government aid of any kind, was due to the goodness of other family members, churches and neighbors. Additionally, they were very close to each other, and that helped keep the family together. Already possessed of the resilience to survive, the family developed the tenacity needed to carry them through the next few years.

CHAPTER 4

SETH'S ROMANCE

Tragedy strikes some families and this one was not spared. When Ava was 14, her oldest brother, Alvin, had left home, attended college and gotten a job in education. Seth was 27, was living on his own, and also had finished his education. He had attained a government job helping to build a local levee. Seth was a very quiet, handsome young man who had a passion for horses. He was blond and fair like his father. He was Ava's second-oldest brother. His job and his horse hobby kept him busy. Seth still came to see the family and would bring money to help his mother with the remaining children, just as Alvin did.

He found a local horse club and joined other young people who enjoyed horses. On one trail ride, he was introduced to Rachel, a striking blonde who shared this love of all things equine. She was from a prosperous family who had several rental properties and a new car dealership in a local town. They became enamored with each other almost instantly. His whole life became wrapped up in Rachel. He asked her to marry him. She said yes and he bought her an engagement ring. They began planning their wedding. He wanted to build a home for the two of them and the plan was to marry as soon the home was completed. They found a lot on a small farm and house plans which suited them both. Life was coming together the way he had envisioned.

Seth had made enough money at his new job to buy a new yellow Ford convertible that he would drive home weekly to see his family. When he would arrive, Ava would be anxiously waiting, as he would let her drive the car down the lane and back. At the beginning of the long lane was an orchard where Ava would wait so that she might make three trips down the lane instead of two. One day Ava was waiting and he did not come. She thought he was probably at the new house because it was almost completed and he and Rachel would look at it daily. She started walking down the lane looking for him to arrive when she saw his car at the orchard. She ran to see him, anticipating her drive back, and found him hanging from a tree. There was blood dripping from a hole in his temple. He also had a gun at his feet. Ava started screaming as she ran back toward the house. The two younger brothers could not control her or make any sense of what she was saying, except he was dead at the orchard. The whole family rushed over there. When they brought him down from the tree, they also found a bullet in his head. Clarissa was trying to console Ava, but when Seth's body fell on the ground, she fainted.

He had left a note in his pocket explaining why he had committed suicide. What the family found out, was that Rachel had given him his ring back. Their forthcoming marriage that was waiting on the completion of the house was never to be. The reason she gave for the breakup was that she was pregnant by another man. To make matters worse, the gun belonged to his mother. Because it was unusual for someone to hang and shoot themselves at the same time, they investigated her for his murder. It turned out that was not true, but it hurt Clarissa because she felt there would always be people who would wonder about whether it was. Having no motive for killing her son and her church's support of her character finally cleared her.

Ava suffered what would today be called a "nervous break-down" due to this traumatic occurrence that would take years for her to outgrow. She had barely recovered from being deserted by her father. This terrible shock of losing a brother that she adored caused her to be less interested in doing things with her family. She refused to eat her meals, was rude to her mother, and rejected any task she was asked to do. This caused her to be spanked by her mother and not included in family fun.

The irony of Seth's suicide was that Rachel married the man she said had made her pregnant. But after the baby was born, it was obvious that it was Seth's child. Her husband divorced her. She and her son moved away to California. When her son reached adulthood, he was killed in a hit-and-run accident. His picture was in the local paper and he looked just like Seth.

CHAPTER 5

THE CONSTANTINES

Calvin Constantine was my grandfather on my father's side of the family. He was born the son of a Civil War soldier fighting for the North. His father survived the Civil War but died shortly thereafter of the flu. At the time of Calvin's father's death, he had two sisters, one older and one younger. Their mother, Yvonne, lived twelve more years, and at her death, two of the children were still teenagers. They moved south on the river to another state, as the oldest girl, Susan, was now 22 and had been dating a barge worker who traveled up and down the length of the river monthly. When their mother died, they knew that the property, which was a small farm and house, would be sold. They would need a new place to live. It would take a while for them to receive the money from the sale.

Susan's beau proposed that they ride the barge down river from their home in Illinois to where he lived in Kentucky. He and Susan would get married and he would take care of Susan and help the others find employment. They would all live together in his house until their property sale was completed. Once this happened, the money was to be divided up among the three children by a lawyer. He was appointed to help them handle the legal parts that they were not old enough or educated enough to understand. It was not a lot of money.

They all found work. Calvin, at the age of 13, went to work in a local factory and saved his money. He lived with Susan and her family, and did not have to spend any of his money to live. When he received his inheritance, he put it in the bank. When he was 21, he invested his inheritance and his savings in a small building which was to become his general store. Calvin had been robbed of his childhood and education but he learned through his brother-in law to read, write and do math. Like so many others in this era he learned to value education. Later when he had his family, he wanted all seven of his children to attend school and graduate.

In 1899, Calvin had decided that the river town he lived in was too corrupt and not a good place to raise a religious family. He also loved the idea of raising his own produce and animals and did not believe in commercially processed food items. He wanted an island and planned to clear fifty acres on the highest point to build a house on stilts in case of flood. He had bought the grounds on the island in 1899. He had paid $1.50 an acre to the state for the three hundred acres and had never done anything but look at it, and dream about what he proposed to do to live there. He also needed a wife and family to complete this dream.

The new acreage he had purchased was a beautiful forest. It had virgin timber, cypress, cottonwood and a lot of other hardwoods and nut trees. To this day, in the spring, the wild cucumber vines make it appear as though you are somewhere in prehistoric times. The mist of early morning, floating through the air across the bayou with the sun beginning to reflect off the water, contributes to the feeling you are traveling back in time. Wild fruit such as blackberries, persimmons, wild grapes and mushrooms were readily available. All varieties of game, swamp rabbits, squirrels, deer, turkey, ducks and doves were in abundance. The birds were prolific and included the blue bunting, bluebirds, hummingbirds, finches, hawks and eagles. The problem was how to clear this land to make it habitable without damaging the beauty. He decided that he would have to wait until he had some sons to help him do the work to realize this dream. Once he met Maeve O'Brien, this dream would begin.

CHAPTER 6

MAEVE O'BRIEN

Maeve O'Brien was a four-foot-ten woman of Irish lineage with a sweet disposition who would later become my grandmother. Her father's family was Catholic and had come from the East Coast with a migrating group looking for land and adventure. Her Irish father, Tom, found a manual-labor job in the same river town where Calvin Constantine lived. Tom decided to stay there when the rest of his group moved out west. He met and married a local girl named Ella. Ella had been placed in an insane asylum at one time when she was very young but was later released to a couple in the river town. She had been too "different" from the other children in the ways she acted at school, and may have been autistic. All this led to her being incarcerated. When the asylum became overcrowded, Ella was one of the few who could be released as she was not considered a threat to society. By the time she met her husband, no one spoke of the problems she had experienced in the past. They married and only had one child, Maeve. The family practiced his Catholic religion at home as there was no Catholic Church nearby. This only child was taught religion and how to read and write by her father, but she had no formal schooling. She was taught by her mother all the things a woman needed to be a wife and mother, which was typical of the times.

Maeve was married at the age of 14, to Grandfather Calvin Constantine who was 39 years old. Calvin had been married twice before and both wives had died in childbirth. One of the babies, a girl, had survived but was being raised by another family member. The other baby and mother had not survived. He wanted a family and had watched this young, pretty Irish girl when her family would come to his general store to shop.

Calvin Constantine approached Tom about marrying Maeve. He knew the family was very poor and offered them a wonderful opportunity to have a better life. Calvin continued talking to Maeve's father and mother for over six months trying to convince them of his sincerity. He offered to build a new house next to his home for Tom and Ella. He told them they would not have to pay anything for it. He also offered them some livestock. Maeve never knew anything about this until the day they were married. Her parents knew he could support her and they were desperate for his help, so they gave their approval. Even though Calvin was not a Catholic and Maeve's father knew that, he still consented. Calvin had told her father that he attended church regularly and Maeve would also. Since there was no Catholic church nearby, perhaps this was consoling to her parents.

CHAPTER 7

GRANDMOTHER MAEVE CONSTANTINE'S STORY

When I was a teenager, I went to "Little Momma's" house to help her clean and paint some furniture. I had never had an opportunity to talk to her alone as she was always surrounded by other grandchildren who lived nearby. I knew a lot about my Grandfather Constantine's family because of a biology class I had in high school. We had a project studying genetics, that involved picking a family member, and finding out as much as you could about your ancestors. Grandfather Constantine was the oldest member of the family at 89 years old, but had a wonderful mind and recall of his family, so I selected him. I told him what I would like to do and he was very receptive. I wrote down all he told me for my project. I had not asked about my grandmother's life, only the ancestors on his side.

I knew very little about Grandmother Constantine's family. She had always been such a sweet, quiet lady. During the few hours we were together, she was sitting under a tree in the yard and I was painting the furniture. I will never forget that day. It was a beautiful fall day and I decided to ask how she had met Grandfather Constantine. She told me, "No one has ever asked me that before. Are you sure you want to know?"

I said of course I would. Once she started, I was shocked to hear what she had to say. I stopped her and said, "I would like to put this on paper. Do you mind?"

Her response was "No," and I went into the house to get paper and pencil to record her words as accurately as possible.

She told me that early one morning, when she was 14, her father came into her room to wake her up. She said these were his exact words and she would never forget them: "Get up, daughter, take a bath and wash your hair. Then put on your white dress. You're getting married today." She was so sleepy and shocked that she did not get a chance to ask any questions. Then he walked out of the room. She did as she was told and then sat down in a rocking chair in her room and cried for about an hour. When her mother called her to breakfast, she finally got a chance to ask her who she was marrying.

Her mother said, "Mr. Constantine, who owns the general store on the bluff overlooking the river."

Maeve said angrily, "I don't want to get married. I don't know him and I don't want to leave home."

Her mother replied, "He is building your father and me a house next to his on the ridge. We will be close by, so don't worry."

With that said, her mother walked out of the kitchen. Without touching her breakfast, Maeve went back to her room and began to rock again. The day seemed so long; lunchtime came and Maeve ate with her mother. He had not shown up, so she began to hope he had changed his mind.

Early that afternoon, Calvin came to the house in his buckboard to pick up Maeve. She vaguely recognized him as the general store owner, as she had never paid much attention to him while they were shopping. She did recognize him as a man who had come by the house several times, when she was sitting on the porch, and had always waved to her. But to her he was an old man, being twenty-five years her senior. He had a large bushy mustache and hair that was just beginning to gray around the temples. He had bright blue eyes which seem to sparkle in the sun. He was dressed in a suit and had on a shirt with a detachable collar that was held in place at the neck by a large button (a man could wear a white shirt over and over and just put on a clean collar by placing the two button holes over the large button). Then he could add a tie if he needed to dress up. This was a special occasion and he had a tie on for his wedding. He introduced himself to Maeve and when she stood up, he led her off the porch and helped her onto the buckboard.

Very little was said on the way into town. Maeve's mother and father went with them, in their own buckboard, to the courthouse to apply for the marriage license, and to sign their permission for this marriage. Once this was completed, Calvin had asked a preacher to marry them in his small church.

At the church, Maeve stood in a daze as they went through the ceremony. They were pronounced man and wife, he kissed her lightly on the cheek, and they walked out of the church. Her mother and father hugged her and her dad shook hands with Calvin. She was very distressed when her parents left and was fighting back tears. As Calvin helped her up onto the buckboard, she watched her parents ride off without looking back. She and Calvin left town and began the ascent to his home that he had built in the hills.

The location of the house looked down on the town where his general store was located. The house was very nice. He showed her where the house for her parents was being built next door. The foundation had already been laid and the livestock was in a corral behind the house. She realized then that this marriage had been planned for a long time, even though she'd known nothing about it.

Once inside, he told Maeve that he and she would get to

know each other the first month. For the time being, he would sleep in another room. As they got acquainted, she found out that he was shocked her parents had not told her about the arranged marriage. On her first night of marriage, before she went to bed, he told her that the house was her responsibility, and he expected three meals a day starting the next day. He also told her that he had two previous wives who died in childbirth and one child being raised by a relative. She lay awake for a long time trying to take in all that had happened that day. The next morning when she got up, she walked into the kitchen to prepare breakfast. She found it fully furnished by his previous wives, as was the rest of the house. Thus, her unusual life began as a wife, and two years later, a mother. It took a while for her to forgive her parents.

Now that Grandmother had finished her story, I had to ask her if she loved Grandfather. She said "Yes, I have grown to love him. He is a kind man." She said he never complained about what she cooked or how she kept the house. He just wanted to be a father and a husband. She said they had not always gotten along, but neither did other married couples.

The family that Calvin had hoped for had come together. In the next few years, he had five boys and two girls. Four of the boys were soon old enough to work on the island. The two older boys cut the large trees while the younger boys cut the smaller ones.

CHAPTER 8

CLEARING THE FOREST ON THE ISLAND

Lyle and his three brothers, Matthew, Mason and Luke had become teenagers, old enough to spend every summer clearing out fifty acres, where they planned to build the house on stilts. They also would be able to farm the remaining ground. They used a 6-foot, two-man crosscut saw to cut the large trees. It was a large, long saw with a handle on both ends. One boy would get on each end and they would pull it back and forth against the tree until it was ready to fall. At that point, all four boys would get on the side where the cut was started and push toward the small attachment of wood on the far side. This was a dangerous thing to do, and Lyle, being the oldest, was in charge of the felling of the trees. Their father would remain at the general store and check on them weekly.

Close to the end of the work, Lyle's father, and a friend of his named Grey, came to view the work the boys were doing. They had just about cut through a tree to prepare it to fall, when a herd of deer came running through the area. Their father and Grey moved to the wrong side of the tree to get out of the way of the deer and the tree began to fall toward Grey. Their father, in a futile attempt, grabbed the tree with both hands to stop it falling on Grey. He must have been firmly gripping the bark, as it ripped off four of his fingernails. The boys reacted by throwing Grey to the ground just in time to have the tree miss him. Grey always attributed his life to being saved by Calvin and not the boys. He said it would have fallen quicker had he not held on to it. Calvin's nails never grew back properly and his fingertips were disfigured for the rest of his life. When anyone asked about his disfigured nails, he loved to tell them about his heroism.

The house area was cleared first to be able to house the boys. They, with the help of a builder, put up a house large enough for the whole family. It was built on stilts on the highest part of the property just like their father had planned. This elevation would keep them from having to evacuate when the river would rise. They had built a large porch across the front of the house with sturdy pillars to tie up the boats. These boats would be needed to row to higher ground. This would enable the boys to walk to buy supplies for the family, if the flooding lingered very long. The family lived there until all the children had grown up. A few years after the children had left, the house burned to the ground, leaving Calvin and Maeve homeless. They moved to the nearest town for the rest of their lives.

The boys' summers of working always involved combat with enormous mosquitoes, and they needed to be protected from Malaria while they worked and slept. They used netting attached to a hat to go over their faces, wore long-sleeved shirts, pants and gloves—which were smothering in the high humidity. Additionally, they had to be protected from chiggers, ticks and snakes. Their pants were tucked into their boots and a rag soaked in coal oil circled around the top. At night they slept under mosquito netting. Other than their boots, there was no need for protection against snakes. There was only one poisonous snake, the cotton-mouth, which was also called the water moccasin. They are pit vipers and have heat-sensing facial pits between their eyes and nostrils. That makes them able to detect a source of heat which is usually prey. They rarely bite humans unless they are provoked. They swim in water and sunbathe on land. They have a narrow neck and a triangular head with a dark line through the eye. Unlike other water snakes, they swim with most of their body on top the water so they are easy to distinguish.

In the fall of the year, the boys attended school back in town. Their father, Calvin, had needed to quit school and go to work at an early age as his father's death left his mother with no income. Calvin did not want his sons to experience the hard life he'd had as a child. Therefore, education took precedence over his dream of the island home.

At the conclusion of the clearing of the ground, the whole family moved to the island. Lyle's dad had saved a lot of money from his general store and other investments. Part of it had been put in a savings and loan. The rest was cash that had been hidden. The savings and loan was one of the first institutions to fail when the Depression of 1929 started. He kept the general store open and thought he could survive it with the cash, but the Depression lasted ten years and the money ran out before it ended. Fortunately, he had bought the land on the island from the government in 1899 and it was paid for. He was forced to sell the general store in the early thirties, so moving to the island was his only option. The Constantines raised their own food, cattle, pigs and chickens. All other meat was acquired by fishing or hunting.

They had a cow for milk, cheese and butter. The way to keep the butter and leftover milk products cool enough was to build a trough filled with water that flowed from a small stream, put the cheese, butter and milk in covered jars and set the jars in it. Meat was smoked for the winter and jerky was also made. Fresh vegetables and jellies were made from the garden and canned. Root vegetables were stored under the house unless the river was up, and then they were placed outside in burlap bags on the porch. Apples were sliced and dried on a low-roofed building and stored.

Kraut was made by the barrel, layering salt and cabbage. It was pressed down tight, and within nine days the brine formed and it was ready to cook. Pumpkin was cut in circles and hung on a broom handle to dry. Once dried, it was put up in sugar sacks and hung in the meat house for future pies. All the other vegetables were canned and all bean varieties were dried and stored. Plenty of bees were available for honey. They grew cane and sugar beets to make sugar. They grew their own popcorn. No food was ever thrown away and no one ever went hungry.

CHAPTER 9

MAKING THE ISLAND INTO A SMALL SETTLEMENT

The island was not the ideal spot for education. Calvin knew he would have to encourage other families to move there in order to have a school. Others had purchased land but had not attempted to clear it. The coming Depression would send these families his way.

Other families who had bought smaller tracts on the island began to build their homes there also. All of these people were remnants of the Depression, looking for a way to survive. They helped each other organize this small community which was very secluded. Finally, Calvin would realize his dream and be able to educate his children too.

Once moved to the house on the island, the children started attending a rural school off the island, a few miles up the road. Lyle and his brother rode a horse daily from the island to school and left it in the woods so no one could see it. He said it was not because there was a fear of theft. The boys felt the horse was so ugly, they were ashamed for anyone to see them ride it. They both were very good students.

Lyle was very talented musically, and could play almost any instrument by ear. He bought his 13-year-old brother a guitar and taught him to play it. While Lyle played the fiddle, his brother played the guitar for the small island community. Every Saturday night they played in local homes where the rugs had been pulled back to make a dance floor. Lyle cut timber during the week and cleared land for his father's farm on the weekends. His father appreciated Lyle's help but did not approve of the music and dancing. He had moved to this island to avoid this same type of sinful living.

Lyle was already too old to change. He was very strong minded and afraid of nothing. He had been involved in fights with other men and attacked by one who had a knife. He had taken the knife away from him and beaten him badly. He would never back down from a fight. His reputation had spread as someone not to anger. He was very respectful to women, but not the best of friends to any man. He instilled fear in a lot of the people who came to the island who were not residents. As there was no law and order, I guess you could say he was the "peacekeeper."

Up the river was a large town. When the town discovered the development on the island, they sent "packet" boats from the cities to service them. Many people had begun to settle on the river and had no access to a store as they were isolated just like Calvin's community. Most of the general stores had been lost in the Depression or were so small that their goods were limited. The packet boats brought mail, dry goods, animal feed and all types of groceries and kitchen supplies. Transportation up and down the river could be purchased for a small fee. Life was becoming more bearable.

CHAPTER 10

PIRACY AND PERFORMANCES

River piracy had been virtually wiped out in the late 1800s on the rivers and canals in the United States. Then in the early 1920s and '30s, a new kind of pirate started discovering these small areas settling in the river. The Pirates were thieves who would come late in the day to these communities and request a place to stay for the night. They always appeared to be jovial, honest people, in need only of shelter and a meal, and willing to pay their hosts. They knew there was no law and order there, so the island communities must have looked like an easy place to rob.

The good-hearted people on Calvin's island would provide a meal for travelers and let them stay. Honest people would show up from time to time requesting the same accommodations and the occupants of the island were happy to have the visit, as well as the money received for providing this service. The islanders frequently put up a tent for the travelers' lodging.

The pirates soon ended the islander's faith in humanity. They had been used to hospitable people up and down this area of the river who were strangers. They had looked forward to them coming to visit and sharing all the news that they were not privy to.

The Pirates would show up on the island, pretending to be good neighbors and requesting an overnight stay and food. Once everyone was asleep, they would plunder all of the belongings in the people's houses and sheds. Easy to do, as most were open due to the warm weather. They would leave before the dawn. If they had adequate rope, they would take the small boats that the residents used to fish for their meals. Then they would work their way up and down the river until they ran out of locations they could ransack.

One summer, the pirates happened upon Lyle's family's island. They came ashore and told them about other places they had stayed on their trips up and down the river. They told how much they had enjoyed visiting and sharing the fine food that was provided. Then one of them said that they had been told that this island was the best place to stop. Lyle asked who told them that, and they said they could not remember the man's name but that he was on the island that was twenty miles downstream. This made Lyle suspicious because the packet-boat captain had told him that there were no organized communities like theirs for at least thirty miles downstream. Lyle decided to spread the word to the other neighbors on the island and they agreed to stay up that night and watch.

After dinner and an extended visit, everyone said goodnight and left to go to bed. It was a pitch-black night where all you could hear was the snoring and noises made by the livestock. Shortly after 1:00 a.m., the pirates, dressed in black, moved from place to place picking up anything of value and placing it in bags they were carrying. Once they were finished, they headed for the river.

The three pirates ran into Lyle, carrying a rifle, as they were preparing to load their bounty into one of the boats they were also stealing. Lyle and the other men on the island tied all three of them to a tree and whipped them. They then left them at the mercy of the mosquitoes overnight. The next morning, they were finally permitted to leave without any firearms or knives they had brought with them. The pirates were told to tell all the other thieves up and down the river not to stop on this island. It must have worked as they were not bothered again. Most of the pirates were not ruthless men, but cowardly ones who were looking for an easy target. This island had not been so easy.

Not all boats were stores on the water. Some paddlewheel boats would come down from the large cities and stop in the larger communities on the way. They would provide music, entertainment and gambling when they docked in a town. They would play loud calliope music as they traversed the choppy river. This would bring everyone to the shore to watch them pass by. They would hang a sign on both sides of the boat telling where their next destination was. It would also give the time and location. Pretty girls dressed in skimpy, colorful costumes would wave from the upper level encouraging everyone to come see the show. This was very entertaining to these people who were so isolated from society. They would dance on the shore until they could no longer hear the music floating across the water. Some of the more religious would call it the "devil's work" and refuse to participate in this sinful exposure.

A few of the islanders could get together enough money to go to the show. After they had viewed the show, they would come home and almost everyone would congregate to listen to their tales of what the spectacle was all about. Some would sing the songs while trying to show the audience how they danced. There was always a lot of laughter watching these amateurs trying to duplicate what they had seen. This show would be a topic of conversation for several weeks with the best parts repeated over and over.

CHAPTER 11

AVA MEETS LYLE

In 1928, Ava was 10 and her sister, Ann, was 15. James, one of her older brothers introduced Ann to Lyle Constantine. Lyle, age 16, was born in 1912 in Kentucky. He was the oldest son of Calvin who was now a general-store owner and part time preacher.

Lyle's worst failing was his weakness for bourbon and beautiful women that started at a young age. He had dated girls on both sides of the river. Many times, he would ride a ferry across the river and walk several miles to court a girl he had met. He was 16 when he came to Ava's home to ask for a date with her sister, Ann. Clarissa knew nothing about him at the time, except that he was good friends with her third son, James. She let Ann date him but he was not Ann's type. Ann had a crush on a Swedish man named Billy, with blond hair and beautiful blue eyes. He was way too old for her. He had come from up north to this part of the country to work on building the river levee. Ann had not mentioned him to Clarissa. Ava, 10, was smitten by Lyle's wavy brunette hair, dark brown eyes and handsome looks. Lyle let Ava sit on his lap and teased her about her freckles and red hair. She developed a crush in that moment that she would never get over.

Seven years later Lyle came back for a date with Ava. Clarissa did not approve of the difference in age, so she would not allow Ava to go out with him. She was very curt with him when he sat down to visit about this date. She thought he was "river trash," and had heard about how he liked to fight and drink liquor. She had tried to keep James from being friends with him. Clarissa was opposed to anyone who came in from the island. A lot of the local people called them "river rats" as they thought they were uneducated and worthless. She had bigger plans for Ava. But the main reason she did not want them to date, was that a local wealthy farmer's son, Eddie Baker, was in love with Ava. The rumor was he wanted to give her an engagement ring and marry her when she graduated from high school. He had been dating Ava and had taken her to several movies and dances. Ava did not know about Lyle asking her mother for permission to date her.

Ava accepted Eddie's ring, which pleased her mother as she wanted her daughters to marry someone with money, as she had done. Even after her experience with being married and deserted by a wealthy man herself, she felt her daughters needed to be courted by someone who could support them. She was proud of the large diamond that Ava had been given and the fact that he was from money. Ava was shocked when she received the diamond and he proposed. Ava liked Eddie, but he was not the kind of man she was looking for. She still thought Lyle was out of reach. Only sister Ann and brother James knew that she was not in love with Eddie.

Lyle told Ava's brother, James, about the experience with Clarissa and how sad he was that he could not date Ava. His heart sank when he was told about her engagement. James said he would talk to his sister and see if she was interested in him. This was passed along to her and she was ecstatic! James helped them to see each other secretly, which allowed Lyle and Ava to fall in love. Lyle knew that Eddie was planning on marrying Ava at the end of graduation from high school. Eddie had told her mother that he would see that she went to college to get her "teaching certificate." Clarissa thought everything was falling in place for her baby daughter.

Two days after her 18th birthday and during her senior year of high school, Lyle proposed. He and she took the river ferry in November, eight days after her 18th birthday, and went to another state to be married by a justice of the peace there. On the way over, Ava had misgivings about this quick marriage and Lyle told her, "if you don't want to get married, jump in and swim back to shore." She laughed and said "You know I can't swim." He said, "Why did you think I took the ferry instead of driving around the long way?"

That night Ava went back to her home with Lyle's ring in her hand. He could not afford a diamond because the Depression had just begun, so he bought her a clear sapphire which looked like a diamond. His timber business income had slowed down with the bad economy. She hid the ring over a curtain rod in the room she shared with Ann. She went to school the next day like nothing had ever changed. Her intention was to graduate in the spring and then announce she was married to Lyle. The problem was she couldn't keep dating Eddie now that she was married, so she gave him his ring back with no explanation. It wasn't long until the secret was out in the public. Clarissa was livid! Ava told her she had to give it back because she had married Lyle. Clarissa said Lyle was just a river rat and that Ava would live and die in poverty married to him. She told Ava she had married trash and she wanted nothing else to do with her. Clarissa told her to get out of the house and never come back! She packed her belongings and left. She was her mother's baby and she was heartbroken.

Ann's boyfriend, Billy, had a car and took Ava to Lyle on the island. His parents were happy for the couple, which was a relief to Ava. She spent the night there and she and Lyle discussed their future. She shed a lot of tears because of her mother's disapproval.

CHAPTER 12

TEACHING IN THE WILD

The next day Lyle and Ava moved from his island home to town. They rented a two-room apartment until Ava could finish high school in the spring. They were young ambitious people and Lyle wanted her to go to college like her family planned. He sent her to a local college where she attended in order to obtain a teaching certificate. Once she had received her diploma, they bought a two-room house in a wilderness area near the river and island where her first teaching assignment was to be located. She was to teach first through eighth grade. The teaching assignment was a one-room school built on stilts with a woodstove for winter and screened windows for summer. She had eighteen students and would teach the oldest first, then have them help with the youngest to learn ABC's and to read. She never allowed anyone to move up a grade until they could prove they knew the present grade curriculum. Some of the eighth graders were as old as 16-18 years of age, and she was only 20. When they left her school, everyone could read and do regular math skills. Very few continued to high school as the nearest was twenty-two miles away and they rarely had the transportation to get there. If you had no relatives you could stay with in town, your chances of completing an education were not good. There was no bus service.

As a teacher, Ava's manner of punishment was peculiar by today's standards. Fighting, which was common among the boys since they were all ages, was hard to control. Instead of paddling, if two boys were hitting each other with their fists and would not stop, she would have older boys take them outside and the whole class would follow. She would then draw a large circle and put the two boys in it. She then would ask who threw the last blow. Whoever had not was the next to hit the other boy. After that, the other boy would hit his opponent again. These blows would go back and forth continuously. Pretty soon someone would have had enough and ask to quit. At that point she would say "No, you boys like to fight and I want you both to continue until you get it out of your system." Soon, both would be begging to quit and she would say, "I have timed how long you two have fought. If you fight again at this school, I will double the amount of time and blows before you can quit." This had a startling effect on all the boys in her class and ceased the fighting until someone new would come to be in her class. They didn't know about this type of punishment unless someone told them, but they would soon learn.

Lyle continued to cut timber for other people during the week, and received a percentage of the timber value when he hauled it to the sawmill. Ava continued to teach. They managed to save enough money to buy forty acres of ground. Lyle cleared part of it for them to plant cucumbers each year. They and some local teenagers picked the cucumbers while they were small. They had a contract to haul their produce to a pickle factory in the city. Both kept saving this money along with their timber money to start a business in the future. They tried to live on her teacher's salary of ninety dollars a month.

CHAPTER 13

UNRULY STUDENT

Then fate dealt Ava and Lyle another blow. Ava had a rough young man in her eighth-grade class who, at 17 years, and over six feet and 200 pounds, refused to do anything she asked him to. He had been sent from another small school in the area because Ava's reputation for discipline had traveled through the small communities. From the first day, he was constantly disrupting the class. When she insisted that he be quiet and follow the lesson, he jumped up, went up to her and slapped her to the floor. She was only five foot two and ninety-eight pounds, and was no match for him. As he knelt over her, he grabbed her right hand. He started to slap her again. She gouged him in the eye with her wedding ring and he pinned her to the floor. All the students appeared to be in shock. The little ones were crying.

Ava had recently had a smallpox vaccination on her thigh and he had knocked the scab off it, wrestling her around on the floor. The blood came quickly through her thin dress. Two of the older big boys saw the blood and thought he was going to kill her. They grabbed him by the arms and pulled him off her. She got up and said, "Bend him over the table!" He struggled to get loose, but the strong boys held him tight. She took a large wooden paddle and hit him as hard as she could for at least a dozen strokes while they held him down. She then told him to go home and not to come back. Then she locked the school door.

She was fearful about leaving the school by herself in case he might be waiting for her. The two boys who had helped her got in the car with her and rode to her home. It was a little two-room house by the levee with two windows, affording scant protection against anyone who might want to enter through the single door. She locked the door and moved the bureau against it and waited for Lyle. She prayed they would not set the house on fire.

When Lyle saw her that night, he was enraged as she had bruises on her face and arms, and blood on her cotton dress. He wanted to hurt the student, but Ava said no. Because he knew the boy and the family, he anticipated that they might come to school the next day to harm her. He first insisted that he would go with her to school. She said, "No, I cannot let people know I am afraid; I will lose my job." He then decided that she should take a gun to school and he showed her how to use it.

The next day she was all bruised and bandaged up when she went to school early to prepare. She laid the gun in the desk drawer and sat down at the desk to arrange her school lessons for the day. Ten minutes later the parents of the young man showed up. There were no other students there at the early time of their arrival. She pulled the gun out of the drawer and laid it in her lap as she knew they could not see behind the desk.

They were furious at Ava, and the father started yelling obscenities at her about whipping their son. The mother screamed that she had left welts all over her son's bottom. Ava was frightened but knew she must remain calm while they vented their anger on her. In a moment of silence following the tirade of the couple, she asked if they wanted to know why he had been paddled? They said he had told them that it was because he did not have his lessons finished. After she told them what had happened and how she had handled it, she added, "My purpose in this small school is to educate your son to read and write and do math. I want him to have a better life. Most of my students never advance into high school and they need these skills to exist. If I can't make him mind me and listen to what I'm trying to teach him, he stands no chance of learning these skills and will never improve his life." They remained quiet and looked at each other. They both stood up abruptly and left the school without saying a word. Ava feared they might get a gun and come back. When she saw all the students coming, she rang the school bell and the rest of the day was as calm as usual.

Next morning, the son and father arrived right before school started. Ava laid the gun back in her lap as they walked in the door. The father said, "My son has come to tell you he is sorry. I want him to learn the things that I never had the chance to learn myself. My wife and I cannot read or write. If he does not mind you and be a good student, come see me as you will not need your paddle. I will take care of him myself."

Ava said," If you and your wife want to learn to read and write, you may come to my house once a week where I will teach you." The man said he would talk to his wife about it. The boy said he was sorry and completed his school year without another problem. His parents took Ava at her word and came on Sunday afternoons for lessons. Before winter came, they were able to read simple books as well as write.

Ava never had another situation that was this bad, but Lyle felt this was too dangerous and wanted her to quit. She said no, but soon had to contend with a different kind of crisis, a flood that washed the school away. Still, she continued on, teaching in a tent that was placed on high ground. Many in her class were also living in a tent. Not one person completed their eight years of schooling without learning all the basics. Some did not graduate from eighth grade until they were older teens. She knew 90 percent would never make it to high school, either because of, as mentioned, the money to attend or the distance to travel. What they needed for their life skills would be up to her and she did not fail them.

CHAPTER 14

THE ENTREPRENEURS

Lyle and Ava continued working and saving, and finally decided to put their money in a tavern along with a dance hall to be open only on the weekends. They called it the Party House. Clarissa had still not spoken to Ava, and if they both were in town shopping, she would turn around and go the other way. This always brought Ava to tears as they had always been so close since her childhood. Their choice of this business further alienated the two.

They hired a retired policeman to keep order, and everyone had a good time and the tavern was a hit. She would greet the customers to collect the cover charge. She always had snack food she had prepared in advance. They had a piano player and a band in which Lyle would sometimes play the fiddle for dancing. Lyle would sell the beer and liquor in the tavern which was attached. He also was the bouncer. They were open on Friday and Saturday nights. She was still teaching and he was still cutting timber, but the tavern was their big moneymaker.

This method of income continued until the seventh year of their marriage when Ava became pregnant in August of 1942. They had been trying for several years and this was a big surprise. They both decided that a tavern would not be suitable employment if they were parents. They sold it and opened a grocery store, which I will tell you about later. The sale was a relief to Ava as Lyle had begun to drink more alcohol since he had it readily available in the tavern.

Ava was not aware of how serious Lyle's drinking problem was until he came home drunk and throwing up from the tavern one evening. She had never seen a man drunk and throwing up and thought he was sick. He passed out so she called the doctor who said, "Hell, Ava, ain't nothing wrong with him except he's drunk. Don't call me out again in the middle of the night!" She was so embarrassed by this, and angry with her husband, that she went to her sister Ann's and spent the night.

They soon became grocers in the front of a house that they converted into a store, with living quarters in the back. As it turned out, the grocery business was not the best way to make a living. Lyle later said "There is more money in vice than groceries."

CHAPTER 15

WAR AND LYDIA ENTERS THE FAMILY

In April of 1943, Lyle received his draft notice along with two of his brothers. Fearful of not coming back from the war and Mother being unable to work since I was due in May, he sold the forty acres and put the money in the bank to help support us before he left for his exam for the service. Hardly anyone was passed up for the draft because the worst part of the war had just begun. When he got there, he was surprised to hear he could not pass the physical because of high blood pressure. His brothers were not so lucky. He was sent home feeling guilty because they had been accepted and he had not. Now the farm and tavern were gone, so he had to come up with another moneymaking idea.

On May 1st, I was born at home in the back of the grocery store to Lyle and Ava Constantine. Daddy had insisted that Mother go to the hospital nearby to have me. She told him that her mother had all her children at home and she wanted to do the same. This turned out to be a grave mistake. It was a breach birth and neither Mother nor I should have survived but we did. The doctor said that I had my arm behind my neck which had saved me from breaking my neck. Being born feet first was hard on my mother. She had a very slow recovery. They named me Lydia and I was the only daughter of a couple who wanted a son. They had already picked out his name and had a hard time making a decision on what to name me. Aunt Ann was thrilled that I was a girl! Daddy soon succumbed to a baby girl's charms. Mother adapted. The best news was that Mother and my Grandmother Clay were reconciled. Getting rid of the tavern, my birth and the scare of the breach birth delivery had reunited them.

My mother was trying to breastfeed me and was unsuccessful. They tried Pet Milk but I was allergic to it. The doctor said I would have to have a specialty milk which was extremely hard to get as well as very expensive. A neighboring state had the formula on what was called the "black market." A black market was established when a company that had access to a product could charge any amount they wanted. The company was in another state so this created another problem: gas. Gas and other petroleum products kept the tanks and battleships moving in the war. Gas was being rationed for the war effort, and only enough was allotted to each family to allow them to go to work, church and town for groceries. The average amount was three gallons a week. There was no extra to just ride around anywhere you wanted. This meant something had to be sacrificed in order to have enough to make the trip for the formula. On several occasions, they did not have enough gas, so Aunt Ann and Uncle Billy would siphon some from their car. They fed me this formula until they were able to wean me.

The government provided limited amounts of items to the public during the war by giving out stamps to redeem for various food and other items. They used war ration books with stamps in them and tokens to give to each family member. The reason was everything from sugar (half a pound per week), to some clothing, had to be sent to the war effort. People donated their pots and pans that were melted for bullets and other ammunition. Scrap drives asked for paper, rubber and rags that were used to build airplanes. When Japan entered the war, it took away the biggest supplier of rubber plants needed for the war, so often people donated their rubber hoses and spare tires. Life was hard, but we were free and determined to remain that way.

My Aunt Ann had to stand on her feet every day at her government job and she required special shoes because she was crippled by an auto accident when she first married. Everyone was rationed one pair of shoes for the year. When I was born, I automatically received my shoe stamps. My parents gave my shoe stamps to Aunt Ann so that she might have a second pair of shoes to help relieve the pain. For the first two years of my life, I went barefooted, until the war ended in 1945. Many children would outgrow their shoes and have to continue wearing them, sometimes with the toes cut out, until the next stamps were received. Everyone had to sacrifice in some way and all were willing to do so to win the war.

CHAPTER 16

DADDY AS BABYSITTER

As loving as my dad was, he never babysat much. His drinking problem had worsened through the years. On one occasion, my mother had to attend a family funeral out of town. He had promised he would take care of me and would not have a drink until she returned. I was 4 months old. Mother had left at eight o'clock that morning because they had a long way to drive to the funeral. By two o'clock, Lyle was drinking some bourbon he had hidden, and he ran out. He looked all over the house in his secret hiding places to find some more, but was not successful. He wanted to go to a local bar downtown to get another drink. Then he recalled he was babysitting. I started crying so he fed me a bottle. That was when he noticed I was wet and needed changing. The one-piece outfit I was wearing had tiny buttons. With his big fingers he could not get it unbuttoned to change my diaper. He'd had enough to drink that he was really not able to function at these tasks. He finally took a knife and cut off my clothes, then attempted to put on a diaper, which fell off and only added to the problem. He could not find any other clothes to put on me, and that tried his patience. The clothes had been laid out by mother with the diapers. Attached was a note instructing how to put on the diaper, but he did not find it.

His craving for a drink was getting stronger, so he wrapped me in the first thing he found: a pair of his pajama bottoms. He carried me to the truck. Once at the bar, he stepped out of the truck, swaddled me in the pajamas and walked in. Everyone in the bar turned around to look, but no one dared to say a word to him because of his rough reputation.

Shortly thereafter, Mother came home and was frantic that we were gone. She drove around town looking for his truck. When she found it, she ran into the bar and saw him sitting on the barstool. She said he had me in his left arm and a drink in his right hand. I was sound asleep. I didn't have a diaper on so I had wet on my father's pajama bottoms plus the pants he was wearing. She was furious about the way I was dressed and was embarrassed by all the attention we were getting from the bar occupants.

My daddy was not concerned about his wet clothes. He was concerned about the chastising he was receiving in front of everyone in the bar. He told her to go home and handed my naked body to her. She wrapped me in her arms and marched out the door. All she could think about was how it would be all over town that he had taken me out in public naked. She was right. This gossip traveled the small town quickly. She packed up all of our clothes and the two of us went to stay for three days with Aunt Ann.

Not a word was said as Lyle picked up his wet pajama bottoms from the bar floor. He left the bar a few hours later. He was so mellow from the drinking that he may never have realized what had transpired that day. When he got home and discovered no one there, he went to bed. The next morning, he went to see Aunt Ann and begged Mother to come home. Once again, he told Mother he'd quit drinking, and once again, she believed him.

CHAPTER 17

MY FIRST IMPRESSIONS OF THE WORLD

Have you ever thought about the first time that you remember being in this world? Were you 3, 4 or 5 years of age? Was it an event that was highly memorable or just an ordinary day? I have often pondered this and am amazed at what I found when I really researched it. One article I read said your first memory could be around 2 1/2 to 4 years old. Another said the hippocampus, a part of the brain found in the temporal lobe, is ready to remember things at about the age of 4. It also said 3-year-olds may remember trauma and nursery rhymes. An article on childhood development said "Memories that are suffused with emotion and fit into a greater context are more likely to form earlier and last longer." Perhaps some of these examples affected the way I remembered things from my early childhood.

An only child's life can go many directions. My life as an only child was definitely different. I spent a lot of time alone including the three months of isolation in the hospital, with an illness. I learned to entertain myself. I cannot say that I was particularly spoiled by my parents, as they always seemed to have high expectations for me. I never went anywhere with them that I was not expected to sit between them and be quiet. I also had to practice good manners with adults and say yes ma'am, no sir, please, thank you, etc. Being respectful to others was most important for a child then, as it should be now.

I was rarely given money, but instead was expected to work for money that was to be used "frivolously." That would include movies, carnivals and candy. I was expected to make A's in school. I believe that parents of only-children expect so much more academically, because they only have one chance to show their family and others that they are good parents.

People always assume that an only child is spoiled and given everything they ask for. That was not the case for my parents when I was young. As they were both from large families and received small gifts for Christmas as well as birthdays, they thought that was the traditional thing to do. Christmas always allowed Santa to bring me a doll along with a basket of fresh oranges and apples. On top would be a box of cookies and a few pieces of chocolate candy. I had no interest in my doll, because my boy playmates teased me about it. Another problem was I so rarely played with other girls, that I wasn't sure what to do with her. I always received one gift from my parents and one gift from my Aunt Ann and Uncle Billy.

My favorite Christmas was the time I received a drum from my parents and a coloring book and paper doll book from Aunt Ann and Uncle Billy. Paper dolls were not something you could easily punch out like the perforated ones today. Instead, you had to use scissors to cut out the doll made of heavy paper, plus all the clothing items that were included in the book. The clothing items all had tabs along the edges. If you didn't cut the tabs properly, they were not going to be long enough for you to fold over the doll so they would stay on her. It was a tedious job but entertained me a lot longer than the drum, since you could change the doll's clothes over and over. My parents didn't take long to figure out they had made a mistake with the drum. The noise was unbearable in the small house.

My grandparents had so many grandchildren that they did not give gifts. Instead, they sent a Christmas card with an occasional dollar bill in it, which was exciting because I rarely got mail. My many cousins were scattered all over the United States so we rarely got together for any special occasions.

When I had a birthday, again it was the same routine every year. I received children's books and comic books. Mother made a chocolate cake and iced it with chocolate icing. There was no ice cream because the icebox was not cold enough to keep the ice cream from melting. On my 8th birthday, we were in the new house and had vanilla ice cream with the cake for the very first time.

When I was older, Aunt Ann told me that my mother was disappointed in my sex and jealous of any attention ever paid to me. I think she was not being mean about Mother, but trying to make me understand why Mother acted so distant. My dad wanted me to call her Momma, and when I did the first time, she was furious. She turned to Daddy and said, "Don't call me Momma in front of her. I want her to call me Mother." At the time I was too little to say Mother correctly so I called her Ava. Later her name became Mother.

Ava never played a game with me, taught me how to play dolls, how to make cookies or take the time to read a book to me. There was no closeness created by anything that involved a "one on one" situation. She would put me in bed and say, "Good night." Sometimes she would kiss me and other times she would just walk off.

She would set me down to learn to read and write. Once she had explained what I was to do, I was expected to learn these things and entertain myself. Daddy, when he was sober, would do things with me, but they were more things that a boy might want to do than a girl. I was always in yearly school plays in elementary school and was a baton twirler with other little girls. I felt Mother liked for me to do that sort of thing to assure the family and all who knew her that she was a good mother. She would always attend anything I was participating in. Perhaps she thought the community needed to see us as a normal family. Daddy never attended anything. I never dwelled on the lack of attention or the loneliness, but did notice that other children's lives were different.

The only time I felt really lonely was yearly on the Fourth of July when I was over 8 years old. All of my friends would be somewhere with their family watching fireworks. I would ask my parents about going to watch fireworks with me. When it was dark, they would say, "Go out by the henhouse and climb up on the fence and you can see all the fireworks you'll ever want to see." I would sit on the fence with the chickens making their chicken noises and watch the fireworks show by myself. What I really wanted was someone to share that special time with.

Mother was so used to being the center of attention and having everybody rave about her beauty. She never walked by men that they wouldn't turn and stare. She had dark auburn hair and flawless skin. She dressed to show her best features even when she was in work clothes. She was very aware of the impact she had on men and flirted with those she found attractive.

Regarding my own light golden-blonde natural curly hair and dark brown eyes, people would often say, "What a beautiful child." From when I was little, I have always remembered my mother's response, which was, "I don't think she's pretty, but she does look intelligent." When people would tell me I was pretty or I had pretty brown eyes, instead of "thank you," my response was always, "Dandy's pretty, too." Dandy was one of three blond Cocker Spaniels that were our pets. As I had always been told I looked intelligent, I never thought of myself as pretty. I didn't know what looking intelligent meant. My daddy once said that Dandy was really an intelligent dog. If Dandy could be that word, I was pleased that I was intelligent, too. My daddy loved me dearly and thought I was beautiful. Without him and Mother's sister, Ann, I suppose I could have developed really low self-esteem.

CHAPTER 18

THE LOVE OF DOGS

Dogs played a big part in my life. One of the first faces I remember was Dandy's. I do not remember how we lost Dandy, but my mother told me this: The dog went everywhere with me. When I would lie down for a nap, I would put my head on Dandy. You could not tell where Dandy's curly hair and mine began and ended as they were identical in color. When I was 4, we lost him in a terrible accident.

I had developed a problem with my ears which sometimes resulted in convulsions that required a hospital visit twenty-four miles away. Early one morning while Daddy was still relatively sober, I had one of these spells which required that quick trip to the hospital. In the rush to get me loaded in the back seat, Daddy didn't notice Dandy trying to jump in the seat with me, and slammed the door on the dog. The heavy door nearly cut the dog in half. His intestines were hanging out, and he was screaming in agony, and Mother was screaming, too! He needed to be put down, and because of the urgency of the trip, Daddy couldn't take the time to go back in the house to load his gun. He made the quick decision to run over the dog to put him out of his pain. It killed him instantly. I was not awake to see it happen. Mother later said, all the way to the hospital, neither uttered a word. There were no veterinarians in small towns to help during that time frame, and I'm not sure he could have been helped. Daddy had made a decision about what was the most important thing to do and he saved my ears. They put me in the hospital for a few days. Mother stayed and Daddy went back home to bury the dog behind the house. He loved Dandy as much as I did and we had lost our faithful friend.

Dandy was replaced with another blond Cocker which we also named Dandy. We only had the second Dandy about a year when a wealthy man named Cooper accidentally ran over her. He was a customer and longtime friend of my parents. He loved the dog and knew how fond I was of her. He was so upset and kind that he asked if my parents would tell me the dog was lost. He said he would then go to the city and buy an identical dog. It took longer than he expected, but he finally found a dog that fit the size and description in another state.

He brought her to our home and let her out. She was a very good facsimile, but she would not respond to calling her Dandy. I knew she was not my dog, but I didn't say anything because Daddy said, "Maybe she had gone deaf and could not hear." Mother finally told me the truth and, although I was sad, the new dog was great. Mr. Cooper apparently had a bad guilt complex about the dog that he couldn't get over. On my next birthday in May, he gave me a small emerald birthstone ring. I wore it for two years until I had nearly outgrown it. One day on the playground at school, we were playing "Jacks" and another child stepped on my hand, mashing the ring into my finger. The finger began to turn blue and they took me to a friend who had a cutting tool to have it cut off. Mr. Cooper wanted to replace it but my parents turned him down.

CHAPTER 19

STARS IN MY LIFE

When you hear someone say "Careful what you say in front of the children; little pitchers have big ears," it is true. I spent so much of my life alone or with adults that I soaked up everything I heard like a sponge. I was able to entertain myself or find something of interest in what people could consider the most boring circumstances. The characters of my hometown were no different than thousands of small towns in the USA. I just gave these citizens the position of "stars in my life." I found many to be fascinating and few to be dull or mean.

My dog, Dandy, was my first recollection of life. I believe I was around 3 1/2. The grocery store that my parents purchased was my second recollection of life. I remember that there was a candy case where all the candy bars and treats were stored. It sat in the back of the store and you had to walk around it in order to get into the house we lived in. I was about 4 when I walked into the store from the house. I stepped into the back of the candy case and saw the candies. I had just figured out how to open the sliding door to get access to the colorful pieces. I put my hand in and picked out a piece while looking through the front to see where my daddy was. I didn't have to look far because he was looking at me through the front part of the case. "Put it back," he said. My eyes filled up with tears but I didn't let go of my treasure.

There were two customers observing our standoff. One was an old man at the front of the store where the tobacco products were stored in cubicles. The other was a toothless woman named Mabel. As I grew older, I saw the old man come in a lot to buy loose tobacco and papers to roll his own cigarettes and learned his name was Merl. I became acquainted with Mabel as she was also a regular who came to purchase snuff. She would buy it and quickly remove the top, then pull out her bottom lip to put in a "pinch." The tobacco juices would leak out of the corners of her mouth, dribble down her marionette wrinkles and finally settle in the deeper wrinkles on her chin. She was constantly wiping her mouth with the hanky she carried. I'm sure at one time the hanky had been white, but now it was a spotted beige color from constant use.

But that day, they were my saviors. Merl said "I'm in a hurry. Would you wait on me?" Mabel added "My old man is in the car and he'll be tired of waiting, too." Daddy turned around and walked back to wait on them and I escaped to the bedroom, candy in hand. As soon as the customers were gone, Daddy yelled for me and I came in the living room with chocolate candy all over me. I could not get the package open so I had used my teeth to get into the wrapper. In the process of eating it as quickly as I could, I had swallowed some of the paper as well. The chocolate was on my face, my clothes and hands. Instead of being mad, like I thought he would be, Daddy laughed. "Your face looks like Mabel's, he said! Don't ever get candy out of the case; you're too young to start eating candy." That was my first piece of candy. It was the best I have ever eaten. Chocolate is still my favorite.

CHAPTER 20

LIFE BEHIND THE GROCERY STORE

Our grocery/home was heated by a coal stove in the living room and a second one in the store. We had a pitcher pump for water to the sink inside the kitchen. This pump had to be "primed" daily to start the water flowing up from under the ground. You did this by pumping the handle as you poured in water which brought the groundwater into the pump. My mother cooked on a gas stove and had an "icebox." A local ice company delivered a block of ice for it twice a week to keep the food cold. We had no indoor bathroom, so Daddy constructed an outhouse with a bench that had two holes cut in it (I always wondered about the two holes as I never could understand why two people might want to share this intimate experience). When the weather wouldn't allow us to make the trip to the outhouse or if we had to go at night, we had a "chamber pot" under the bed which we used and covered up. This was emptied and cleaned out daily.

Once a week, my mother would fill up a galvanized tub with water that she had pumped into a pot and then heated on the stove. Then she would carry the hot water to the tub. Next, she would add cold water to make it just the right temperature. I was the first to get a bath. After my bath, Mother and Daddy would take turns using the same bathwater. More hot water would be added each time as it cooled off. It was much too hard to carry the weight of the water to pour out after each bath. During the winter, this tub was placed next to the coal stove to keep you warm while you bathed. In between baths, you took a sponge bath, cleaning your body in all the "special" areas.

CHAPTER 21

DADDY'S NEW BUSINESS

In 1947, my daddy got an opportunity to open a farm equipment dealership. The money he had saved from the sale of the forty-acre farm, when he was drafted, was finally being used. The tavern sale money they had saved had been squandered on the grocery. Lyle built most of the new building with help from his youngest brother, Amos, on the property next to the grocery store. He had the building that housed the tavern removed. Mother became his "parts man" and bookkeeper. Daddy handled the sales of tractors and other pieces of equipment.

The dealership was finally open in 1948. They closed down the grocery which was never profitable, and started selling tractors. They had all their savings invested in this business. The first year didn't go too well as they only sold one tractor all year. Daddy fell into a depression and began drinking more, starting at seven in the morning and finishing a fifth of bourbon by the end of the day. He was getting thinner due to lots of alcohol and little food consumption. Mother chose to ignore his state as she never understood how to help an addiction problem. Her first exposure to anyone who drank happened the second week they were married, so she had no background in what to do or who to ask for help.

This new farm equipment business required owners to attend farm equipment meetings in the nearest large city. They both attended at the end of the first year hoping to visit with other dealers to find out what they might do to improve their business. The first meeting offered assorted gifts given by companies to advertise their products to the dealers. They brought these gifts home. One gift was a deck of playing cards and the other a device that would separate the white of an egg from the yoke. They left them in the living room on the coffee table. The next morning, I got up early and wandered into the living room and saw the white sack. Being curious, I opened it up.

I discovered the contents and was fascinated. I was 5 years old and had never seen playing cards before. I already knew how to read so I sat down to study how to use them. On the box were directions on how to play poker. The first step said to cut the cards in half. I got a pair of scissors and cut each card in half. After that the rest of the directions made no sense, so I opened the box containing the egg separator. The gadget had an indented round center with three holes around it. The directions said to get an egg, hold the separator over the bowl, and place the egg in the middle. It did not mention cracking the egg first. So, I placed the whole egg in the center and waited and waited. The egg did not separate. In an attempt to look under the separator, I lost control of the egg and it fell, missing the bowl, onto the linoleum floor. Knowing my fastidious mother would be upset over the mess, I ran to the clothes hamper and grabbed the first thing I came upon: my mother's new white silk blouse that she had bought for the meeting she had just attended and worn only once. I used it to clean the egg up, and threw it back into the hamper where it managed to drip egg on other items inside.

Daddy soon discovered his new cards had been ruined and Mother saw the remnants of the mess I had made on the floor.

That day, I found out that silk is too slick to absorb a runny egg. Daddy was upset about the new cards and asked me why I did it. When I told them why I had done it, they both laughed and Mother said, "All you were doing was following directions, but the next time you see something that doesn't belong to you, please ask before you touch it." She didn't ask how I cleaned it up, and I didn't volunteer to tell. When she found the blouse later that day, the dripping egg had found its way onto several other items in the hamper. She quit laughing.

CHAPTER 22

ILLNESS CAUSES BUSINESS CHANGE

Daddy's drinking binge continued into the next year. In the winter of 1948, he began to spit up blood. The diagnosis came back saying he had tuberculosis. He had contracted the disease from his youngest sister who had lived in our home temporarily while she finished high school in town. There still were no buses to bring her the twenty-two miles into town to school. Fortunately, my mother's immune system never allowed her to catch the disease. Since I was 4, Daddy was bedfast with tuberculosis and had been in and out of three hospitals where he had not been able to recover. His constant drinking had suppressed his appetite and his immune system suffered. The beginning of the deterioration of his left lung had started. The new drug, streptomycin, which had been discovered in 1943, was not used until November of 1944. It reached the rural communities much later. He went to many doctors and spent time in and out of city hospitals, being treated with this new drug. In between hospitals, he spent time in what had been my bedroom in isolation. During that time, I would sleep in bed with my mother, and neither she nor I could go into Daddy's room without face masks and gloves.

She gave him his "strep" shots daily while also becoming our sole provider in the farm equipment business.

Mother realized that she was not a salesman, and that keeping the books as well as manning the parts department was all she could handle. She hired a salesman who took Daddy's job and began to move the inventory. In the last few years, Daddy was only effective in sales in the morning hours when he was working. By noon he was too drunk to promote the business. At five o'clock he would finish the day drinking with the business owner next door who was also his tractor sales competitor, T.J. Denton. Mother continued to work the parts counter daily while handling the money. Business began to improve.

Mother's biggest problem in the business was getting people to pay their bills. Since she was a woman, I suppose they thought that she would be unable to collect their money, so they just ignored her billing. She wanted to ask for the money but every time she mentioned it to Daddy, he would say, "I'll take care of it when I get better."

She was running short of money to keep the business going, and after looking at the books, she said to me, "Get in the car, we're going to get some money from these people who owe us. I wasn't sure how she intended to do this, but after she stopped at the first two houses and was successful, she became braver. She would say "I'm here to collect what you owe me on your farm equipment account." Some were rude and she would say, "I can't live without this income; my husband is bedfast and I am running this business and trying to be a wife and mother. Our medical bills are more than our income and we barely have enough to buy groceries."

I'm sure we looked pitiful standing on their front porch begging for money. If there was a woman in the house, she would encourage her husband to help us. Most customers would be sympathetic and either pay part or all of the bill. We continued doing this nightly for one week each month. Sometimes we would go back to the people who had paid part of the bill to ask for more.

Mother told me she was waiting until she had collected all the little bills before pursuing Mr. Morgan, who owed the largest account and had not paid for over a year. Once she had finished with the past dues that were relatively easy, a week later, we headed to Mr. Morgan's house. He lived down a dirt road with large trees hanging over both sides. When we reached his house, we were surprised at what we saw.

He owned several hundred acres and was a corn and wheat farmer, plus he had a pig operation. The pigs were inside a fence which was around his house. You had to walk through the front yard with the pigs running back and forth to get to the front door. The odor of the pig manure was overpowering. It is such a strong smell that it hurts your nostrils. When you opened the gate, all the little pigs came running, excited to see you. They were cute, but closely followed by the big sows who were neither cute nor friendly. The sows would run up to you and place their mud-encrusted snouts as close as possible to you. All the while, they were making a snorting sound. I was scared of them because I thought they wanted to bite me. I was hanging on mother's leg and hiding under her dress. Mother picked me up and stepped onto the porch. The whole time she was talking to Mr. Morgan, I was worrying about the trip back to the car without being eaten by the sows.

Mother told Mr. Morgan the purpose of her trip, and he said he couldn't pay her anything because he didn't have any money. Mother said "You have a lot of pigs that look old enough to sell. What are they worth?" He told her their value which I don't recall, because I was wanting to go home. Mother said, "I see four that I think would be enough to pay your bill to me if you are willing to let me have them." He said, "If you think you can take those four hogs and sell them, you'll have to come get them. I'm not helping you." He then closed the door in her face. She carried me back through the hogs to the car. We both smelled like them because we had waded through the manure and my feet had spread the manure all over my mother's dress.

When we got home, I thought she would clean us both up but it didn't happen. She drove right past our house and directly to the mechanic, Sherman's, house and she told him the story. He came and got our shop pickup truck and we all three went back to Mr. Morgan's. I stayed in the truck while she and Sherman loaded the pigs. Mr. Morgan was mad because he didn't think she would come back. She told him that if he was a man of his word, he should let her have the pigs. Surprisingly, he did. The next day she sold them and made more than what she thought.

Later in life, I found out that I was right to be afraid of the sows. A local farmer died while feeding them, and when they found his body, the sows had feasted on it.

CHAPTER 23

LYDIA'S ILLNESS

Early winter 1948, when I was 5, I had contracted the mumps. After the swelling in my cheeks went down, I was finally allowed out to play with friends, as the contagious phase was over. Letting me out early turned out to be a mistake a few days later. I developed what they thought was appendicitis. This problem sent me to the hospital and, upon examining me, they determined that I did not have appendicitis, I had complications from the mumps which had settled in my ovaries. I also got double pneumonia.

The small hospital had a children's ward which housed about ten children. There was just a rail and glass partition between the next bed and myself. A girl named Marla was in a tent lying on her stomach. She was being treated for severe burns to the back of her body. Her father tanned animal hides and she had received these burns by falling backward into a vat of boiling water, that her father had used to tan the hides. She was very vivacious and was happy to have someone to talk to. As an only child with no girlfriends, I enjoyed her company as we were the same age. Unfortunately, that time was short-lived because I had to be moved.

When they checked my x-rays, they discovered that I too had tuberculosis. This caused me to be placed in isolation for three months in a small single hospital room. They could not allow me to pass my disease to other people in the ward. I was upset when they put me in the room by myself before they walked out and closed the door. I was not afraid, but I hated the smallness of the room with only one outside window and a door with a window where people would stand to stare at me, but would not come in. No one was allowed to visit me in isolation except for my parents. Daddy was in the hospital and Mother was working every day. Because I had only a working mother to visit me, the hospital relaxed their strict rules and allowed Aunt Ann with her husband, Uncle Billy, to visit me. Three months is an eternity for a 5-year-old child. Everyone felt sorry for me and tried to think of things for me to do.

My schoolteacher mother had taught me my ABC's when I was 4, and by age 5, I could read and write. The people who lived in the small town I grew up in were so kind to me. They would send me children's books to read, crayons, coloring books and paper dolls. I was forced to take a nap every day, while some days I had to go for tests and x-rays. My medication was two shots of streptomycin a day. I hated the shots as the needles were larger than the types that are used now, plus they always left a bruise.

I was still in isolation at Easter, and was very concerned about the Easter Bunny finding me. I asked my nurse named Mrs. Cook if someone could please let the Easter Bunny in the isolation room to see me, or would he get sick? Mrs. Cook said she was not sure, but would see if she could find out.

On Easter morning, I got out of bed and searched all over for the eggs. There were no Easter Eggs to hunt in the small room, which made me disappointed. A few minutes later, when the meal tray came in, it was covered with stuffed Easter bunnies, candy eggs, a small chocolate bunny, lots of books and an assortment of Easter cards. I was so excited! All this was from the nurses, the doctor and the people who lived in my hometown. I always thought I was blessed to have grown up in a town where everybody knew and cared for me. I was grateful to my nurses and doctors, too. This was my first introduction to the kindness of people who were not related to me.

CHAPTER 24

BURNING THE CANDLE AT BOTH ENDS

During my isolation, my mother was running the business and struggling to help Daddy with his needs, so she could only visit me after work. She would come to tuck me in at night. The hospital was twenty-four miles from our home so she was on the road a lot. Aunt Ann also worked, but she would come to see me anytime Mother could not. Shortly after I entered isolation, Mother developed the mumps. She wore a headscarf in public so people could not see the mumps swelling. She had to open the business every day. During this time, a customer came in who wanted to see a piece of equipment that was in the yard. The salesman was not working because he had to take his wife to the dentist. He told Mother where the piece of equipment was and she proceeded to take the customer out to look at it. When she turned around to go back into the business office, she tripped over a plow and broke her leg. Tough as she was, I can't imagine being at work, walking on the concrete floors with a broken leg while feeling bad from the mumps. Plus having two sick family members depending on her.

She had barely recovered from the mumps and gotten the cast off when Daddy's health began to deteriorate further. The local doctor had put him back in the hospital where they told him he needed to have his lung removed due to the tuberculosis destroying his lung tissue. They said it was imperative that he have the operation within the next few days.

Daddy was fearful of losing the lung. Someone had told him about a doctor from Europe who was practicing at the state sanitorium for lung diseases. This doctor treated the disease differently and they had more modern equipment there. The sanitorium had embraced the "Open Air and Rest Program." The windows were always open so that the patients were not confined with the germs. When the room became unbearably cold, the patients were given flannel pajamas, heavy socks, bonnets to sleep in, extra cover and sometimes hot-water bottles. There was no relief in the summers from the heat and humidity with the windows open. The hospital provided fans on both ends of the "veranda" and in the center. The beds were all lined up in a row. Some of the buildings had as many as thirty beds in a row, and the area they called the "out building" had only eight beds in a row. There were few private rooms which were only for people with highly contagious problems. Many of these had to be shared by two patients.

The streptomycin that Daddy had been taking was also administered along with this program. In addition, they had special cows whose milk was high in magnesium. They were finding out things about nutrition that seemed to help improve their patients' health, and magnesium intake was one of them. These cows were raised on the property and their milk was served at every meal. All these new ideas seemed to be boosting the patients' health and energy.

Daddy, fearing that he would not be able to get out of the local hospital and to the sanitorium in time, had someone call Mother. He told her he was scared and he thought the sanitorium might save his lung and his life. He told her to pick him up at the hospital now! He wanted to see if they could drive to this location in time to save his life without taking out his lung. He was very sick at this time. She left the business with the new salesman and me in the hospital, to take him there. Aunt Ann was left in charge of me. Mother drove the twenty-four miles from the farm equipment business to pick him up, on what turned out to be one of the worst winter days that year. The local hospital put Daddy in the back seat, resting his head on pillows, as he was having problems breathing. It was very cold, so they covered him up with blankets, and gave him a container of water to drink. Mother had not thought about bringing any food because she was in such a rush to pick him up, and she thought they would be at the sanitorium in about five hours.

CHAPTER 25

TREACHOUS TRIP

My parents started across the flat country toward the hospital, but as soon as she reached the hills toward her destination, it began to sleet and snow. From this point, the trip was through a forest. It was 235 miles of two-lane roads. In good weather the trip took five to six hours. The further she went, the thicker the sleet and snow became. The snow was beginning to cover the roads,which was good because the sleet had it made it slick. It was also going to be dark soon.

About halfway there, a state trooper had closed off the road and told her she must turn around and go back to the last town and spend the night. She told him her story about Daddy and began to cry uncontrollably. She said, "If I go back, I won't have a husband alive tomorrow." He said he would call ahead to see that she made it to the next town. There would be law enforcement of some kind at every stop. They would relay the call from town to town, all along the way until she reached her destination.

From that point on, the visibility was terrible and she only progressed less than twenty miles an hour. She could not tell where the edge of the road was and tried to stay in what she thought was the middle. Two times she came close to not making it as the car slid off the road. She came across a bus that was off the road and tried to go around it. When she tried to bypass the bus, it was the first time she slid into a ditch. Two men got out of the bus to see if she was all right. She told them her dilemma. They returned to the bus and told the passengers. Having heard her story, several men came to her aid and pushed the car out of the ditch. She thanked them and immediately continued on down the dangerous road.

Several miles down the road she misjudged the edge of the highway and slid into the ditch a second time. This time she thought the trip was ended as there was no one to help her. After a few minutes she saw the headlights of a large truck. The driver stopped and hooked up to the car with a chain to pull her out. Again, she expressed how thankful she was and continued on her way. When she had arrived in the few towns along this route, someone with law enforcement would be waiting for her as they had received the message that was being relayed. They would clean her windshield, headlights and windows. Many offered prayers. When they reached the last checkpoint, someone handed her two sandwiches with coffee. She was grateful for the food because she had been on the road for over twelve hours. She turned around to offer some food to Daddy, but he was asleep or passed out. She started crying because she was afraid he might be dead. She did not step out of the car to check him because she feared falling and the broken leg had just gotten the cast off.

They finally arrived at the hospital. The state patrol had called the hospital to make sure they were waiting for him. He was immediately taken to emergency care for treatment. Mother was so exhausted, she fell asleep in the waiting room. It was worth the trip! The European doctor proved to be as good as his reputation. Daddy was able to keep his lung, except for the part that had been eaten away by the tuberculosis. He was hospitalized for several months until he was strong enough to return home. What was left of his lung that hadn't been eaten away was about the size of a large orange, but it was functional. Mother stayed at the hospital with him that initial night until the roads were clear, and then returned home the next day.

CHAPTER 26

LYDIA IMPROVES AS DADDY WORSENS

After leaving the hospital shortly, following the third month, I was sent home to recuperate. I stayed with Mother for a few weeks and made the long trip once a month to the sanitorium to see my daddy. They allowed him to come out to the car and talk to me through the glass. He was so happy to see me and I always wanted him to hug me. That couldn't happen because of both our TB problems. It was such a highly contagious disease that Mother was fearful I would get it again, even though Daddy was doing a lot better. He was living in a hospital building with other men who were still harboring the disease. The good news was, he had not had a drink of alcohol since he had arrived. Mother was hopeful that this would cure him of the alcoholism. It was important that he give up the alcohol and continue to eat a good diet after he returned home in order for his health to return. The disease had eaten his fat reserve up, aided by the excessive alcohol consumption. Daddy was forty-five pounds underweight. He could not leave the hospital until he finished his medications and gained the weight back. He would also have to test negative when the TB sputum test was given, and his x-rays would have to be clear of the disease.

What to do with me remained a problem for my mother during the time I was in the hospital. She was running the business and seeing me nightly in the hospital twenty-four miles from our home. On Friday nights, she would wait until I fell asleep before driving the 258 miles to spend time with Daddy on the weekends. She would leave him on Sunday afternoons and drive home. She would come to see me on the way back before going home to bed. She was leading a hard life that no other mother in my hometown could match. She was not sure once I was out of the hospital how she was going to rearrange our lives. One time Mother said that during that turmoil, she would wake up every morning and just deal with each day at a time. She just wanted to hold up until it was all over. At least for this period of time, she did not have to deal with Daddy's alcohol problem.

CHAPTER 27

SUMMER TRIP 1949

The summer of 1949, Mother and Aunt Ann wanted to go to California to visit their mother. Clarissa had married Daniel, a World War I veteran, the year Ava had left home. Clarissa had relatives living in California, and upon visiting them decided that she would spend every winter in the warmer climate. She and her husband, instead of coming home from California in the summer like they had done for two previous visits, decided to stay all year. She had taken a job with a local ladies' club as their chef. She had no credentials showing she was a chef. She sent the ladies her resume and asked if she might bring a sample of her cooking. She had always been a fabulous cook, and often invented recipes that were really different. Once the club tasted her food, they hired her. Daniel started mowing yards, which were very small lots, with a reel mower. Soon he had an additional income that allowed them to be comfortable. They had purchased a small two-bedroom house in a modest neighborhood.

Aunt Ann and Mother were homesick for their mother, Clarissa, and Uncle Billy had just gotten a new 1949 gray Plymouth. He thought the time to make the long trip to visit her was now, while the car was new. Daddy had been released from the hospital and was trying to stay sober. He felt Mother needed a break and encouraged the trip. Her only worry was that he might start drinking again if she left, but he insisted that he was cured after the long stay in the hospital. She decided to take me along on the trip.

It was the beginning of summer vacation. When we left, Daddy looked so low and Mother looked so unhappy. I was excited about going out west to see the Indian reservations and all the other things I had been told about. Aunt Ann had planned a long trip that was to last six weeks. We were to go to Claremore, Oklahoma, to see the Will Rogers Museum, Grand Canyon National Park in Arizona, and Carlsbad Caverns in New Mexico. Then we would be in California where Grandmother Clay had plans for us to see all the famous sights around the town of Orange where she lived, then go across the border to Mexico.

There was no air-conditioning in the cars in 1949. Many hotels and restaurants did not have cooling units in our home state, but we expected to experience air-conditioning in these warmer states. Once we left Oklahoma, headed southwest through Texas, the weather began to warm up a lot. The sun would beat down on us in the car. Our only protection was an umbrella that Mother opened up and positioned so that we had a little shade. All the windows were rolled down, and you had to be careful where you placed the umbrella so that you didn't block the breeze coming in and the umbrella didn't fly out the window. Everyone had a paper fan to fan themselves but it was miserably hot. The air coming in the windows was like a blast from a hot furnace. We would get up early in order to travel as far as possible before noon. We carried large amounts of drinking water with ice in it until we got further west where there was little ice to be purchased. The ice did not last long in the heat. Most days the temperature was over 100 degrees by noon.

When we got to New Mexico we stopped at a gas station to get gas plus something to drink. The serviceman told Uncle Billy that he needed to buy this special bag that he could fill with water and hang on the front of the car. The purpose was to have water handy if the radiator got too hot, which frequently happened going across the desert. There were very few places to stop for water and gas going west. They had signs that would warn you about how far it was to the next stop. The farther west we went, the more intense the heat became. There was a lack of any breeze, except air being pushed into the car due to the speed we were making. That night, when we stopped, was the first time we had a room with an air conditioner. Mother washed out all the clothes we had in the sink early that morning before we left. There were no facilities in the hotel for doing laundry.

Once Mother got in the car, she would tie a small rope on the two or three items, then tie the rope on both ends to the coat hanger and door handle. She would then hang them out the window to dry. The heat and the wind would dry them almost immediately. They would be flapping in the breeze which made an annoying sound, but you had no choice but to listen to it. Next, she would put more items out until she dried all the laundry. Sometimes the clothing would fly off the rope and we would have to go back to find it. Fortunately, there was little traffic, so the clothes were not covering someone's windshield behind us, or being run over by a following car leaving tire tracks on the clean items. Uncle Billy had been in the Navy and he announced, "when you hang out the panties plus the boxer shorts in a row, it looks like signal flags." Everyone laughed, but I didn't understand the joke.

The adults would take turns driving, and we would stop for lunch along the way. Lunch was always the same for me. All I ever ate for the past year was the new bread product called "Brown 'N Serve Rolls." I only ate the centers and a serving of French fries. We walked into a diner in Arizona in order that I might have my special meal. They had no air conditioning, so we bought our food to go. Each of us wanted to buy a Coke, which cost 5 cents at home. Here it was 15 cents. We all decided we would just drink water, until we found out it was 25 cents a glass. The reason for the expensive water was explained to us by the owner. All the drinking water in the town had to be brought in from another state. We made the decision to buy two Cokes and two waters that we would share.

After all the traveling and sightseeing, we were happy to cross the California Line. We had seen all the things Aunt Ann had promised except for a few points of interest that would be observed on the return trip. Now we were ready for a two-week stay in Orange. "Big Momma" (Clarissa) was happy to see us and had prepared a big meal for dinner. Mother told her I only ate rolls and French fries. I said, "No I don't," and I ate some of everything she had cooked. I could tell Mother was not happy with me.

We spent the next day touring the town but had to be home before seven that evening, because the next-door neighbor wanted us to come to their house. They had bought a new device called a television. That night there was to be a wrestling match in Los Angeles starring a man called "Gorgeous George." They invited us to watch it. The TV was a square box not much more than twelve by twelve inches. The middle part that was the tube was almost round except for the corners. It was a very small picture so we all sat close together tightly around the screen to get a better look. The TV station was in Los Angeles so the picture was fairly clear with very little snow.

Gorgeous George was a big man who looked really muscular, but a little chubby. He had on wrestling shorts and shoes that matched, and a fancy velvet cape with a feather boa trim. He had long, light platinum-blond hair (it was a black-and-white TV so it was hard to decide if his hair was blond or white). He strutted down the carpeted runway to the arena. In his hair were gold hairpins which he had used curling his hair. He would reach up in there to remove one pin every time he took a step. This would let a curl drop out. Then he would look around to decide on which woman he wished to catch the golden pin. Ladies were yelling and grabbing for the pins, and one even fainted!

After he finally made it to his destination, he stepped into the wrestling ring where an attendant removed the cape with a flourish. Next, the attendant sprayed him with perfume from a fancy atomizer. After blowing kisses to the audience, he then started wrestling his opponent. I really don't remember who won, as the ladies in the audience were more interesting for me to watch than the fight. Some were swooning and waving their hankies at him, while others were fanning themselves like they were hot. They were oohing and aahing when he would look into the audience. They were shouting and crying when he would get knocked down by his opponent. The opponent looked like an ordinary man who had been waiting in the ring the whole time George had been putting on this display. He did not seem to have a fan club and was booed frequently. I had never seen a wrestling match before and felt sorry for the man who had no fans or friends. I also wondered why he had no fancy clothes.

Our hosts were just as excited as the people at the wrestling event. They were very knowledgeable about "Gorgeous," as they called him. They knew how many times he had been married and told us all about the expensive houses he owned and about how his clothing changed at every event. They showed us pictures of his clothes that looked like lady's dresses that he wore in public to special events. They looked strange to me. I had never seen a man dressed this way before. Every one of us enjoyed the special TV program and thanked the host and hostess and returned home to Big Momma's.

I was not aware of what wrestling was, or TV until that night. It made a tremendous impact on me. When we came back home, I wanted a TV. Not only could I not have a TV, we did not have a TV station anywhere near us. I never saw Gorgeous George again. By the time we got a TV set and a station near us, he was no longer an "item." We did eventually get a TV set but the nearest TV station was 150 miles away. Television for the rural areas was very slow in coming.

Not only did the next-door neighbors in California have a TV, they had a long narrow hole, the length of three cars, that ran down the side of their yard, between their house and Big Momma's. There had been a fence erected on both sides of the hole. You could look down it and not see to the bottom. The hole, they said, had been caused by one of many earthquakes California had experienced. I don't know if they were waiting for someone to come fill it or what they planned to do about it, but it was scary to look at.

Grandmother Clay mentioned to my mother that there was a weekly radio program that was very popular in Los Angeles, called *Queen for a Day*. It had originated in New York City, then came to California in 1945. It was a big prize giveaway that entailed submitting your "sob story" about some terrible things that you were presently enduring. The host opened the show with "Would you like to be Queen for a Day? Then the contestants who had been chosen would have their information reviewed by a panel of people. The panel decided which stories were the worst or saddest. If you were selected, you would come forth and tell your story to a live audience. The five stories were always about financial and emotional hard times. Many times, the subject would break down in tears as they explained their misfortune, causing the audience to tear up also. Next the host would ask them what they needed to alleviate this problem. After he had heard from each of the women, he would use an "applause meter" to measure the winner. The highest meter level would be the one to win. The host would then place a velvet robe trimmed with sable around the winner, and a jeweled crown on her head. She was then placed on a throne and given a dozen long-stemmed roses to hold while they announced her prizes. She was given what she had requested and additional sponsor prizes such as a trip, fashionable clothing or a night on the town.

Mother and Aunt Ann were so excited about this show that they sat down and composed a letter about all the hardships that Mother had endured in hopes that she could become part of the show. They went to the radio studio to find out how to turn this information in to become a contestant. They discovered you had to be a part of the audience with your story in hand. The next week Mother, Aunt Ann and Grandmother Clay showed up early in order to get a seat. As you came in the front door you gave them your name and your story. The studio was small and everyone was struggling for a seat so that they might compete. Mother and Aunt Ann squeezed into a seat quickly but Grand-mother Clay was not so lucky. She ended up having to wait outside. Almost an hour later, the show began. I was home with Daniel with the radio on waiting to hear my mother's name called.

They called the five women up to the stage, but Mother was not one of them. They stayed and watched the show to determine if they should return next week. They wondered if there was anyone being called from outside of California and thought they might find that out today. They returned one more time and decided that there were too many sad stories waiting in the audience. They did not return the third time.

We went to Knott's Berry Farm and to another place near Hollywood, where I got to see a horse that looked like Roy Roger's first horse, Trigger. Trigger was a beautiful Palomino and had been stuffed to appear that he was bucking. You could pay to get on his back and have your picture made with a cowboy hat on. I climbed on in my dress and got the cowboy hat. I refused to wear the shoes I had on because they were not cowboy boots. So, in the picture I am barefooted. Next to the room where the horse was displayed, you could purchase souvenirs, including a Roy Rogers outfit complete with hat, or the outfit of his wife, Dale Evans, also including a hat. Daddy had given me money to spend. I decided I wanted to be Dale Evans. I had some boots at home so I thought all I needed was a pair of spurs. They did not have the spurs. I was so excited that I slept in the outfit that night except for the hat.

We visited Long Beach amusement park where I rode the rides and swam in the ocean. The two weeks went by pretty fast. After the first week and a phone call to Daddy, my mother started weeping and told my Aunt Ann that she wanted to get a train and take me home. Aunt Ann told Mother that she could go, but they were keeping me, so that I could experience Mexico, along with the other highlights she had planned for the return trip. Aunt Ann told Mother she would take her to the station the next morning. After sleeping on it, Mother decided to stay. The next day we went into what they called Old Mexico and Aunt Ann bought me a handmade Mexican jacket made from felt and embroidered with all the neat western things such as cactus, etc. I did not spend any of my money there. I was looking for spurs. Mother bought a leather-tooled purse for herself and a tooled billfold for Daddy.

Two nights before our return, we went down to what they called "The Circle." It was a boulevard where you could sit in the middle between the two streets. It was a very upscale neighborhood. Expensive shops were on both sides of the street. On the corner of one of the streets there was a Mexican shop which had silver items in the window. We were walking along that street when I saw them! Silver spurs in the window! They had a clover leaf on them and two stars where they attached to the boot. I told my mother I wanted to buy those spurs. She said, "No, they are probably too expensive." I talked her into going in and asking. They told us how much they were, and they were too expensive.

The salesclerk said they were too big for my little feet anyway. He told us if we'd come back tomorrow, he would see if they couldn't find some children's spurs in the Mexican market.

We came back the next afternoon, and he had a set of spurs with the two stars where they attached. They did not have the clover leaf, but they had a Longhorn steer's head on each one. That was even better. They were still a little too much money. Mother bargained with him and could not get him down to the amount of money I had left from Daddy. She finally gave in to pay the difference herself. I think she was tired of hearing about the spurs and I had worn her down! The spurs were worth it! When I played cowboys and Indians with the boys, they may have all had cap guns, but no one had the jingle of the spurs when they walked. They were jealous.

The return home was exciting as we got to see some of the Indian tribes. I loved their teepees, their ponies and their clothing. They all looked so proud! My Aunt Ann wanted a picture of me with the Indians, but they refused. One Indian who spoke English and was a tour guide told us that they feared the camera image would steal their "spirit" so we didn't get our picture. Instead, we bought Indian beaded jewelry and feathers. We did get to watch the colorful dancing and chanting while the Indian braves beat on their drums. It was my favorite part of the trip back. Now it would be hard to decide when I played with the boys whether to be a cowboy or an Indian.

The next stop was home and I was excited to be there. Daddy was happy to see us when we returned, and I could tell he had missed me. He laughed when he saw what I had done with his money. I believe this was one of the closest times I ever saw between my parents. Even when Daddy was away at the hospital, Mother was always there to see him so he never had a long separation. Six weeks of not seeing her had sobered him up a lot. He hugged her for the longest time when she got out of the car.

Uncle Billy was worn out from the long drive and said it was the last long trip he would ever take. It was a great experience for all of us, but especially for me.

CHAPTER 28

MY FIRST YEAR OF SCHOOL

The time for school came and Mother enrolled me in our hometown school, hoping she would not have to ask Aunt Ann to take care of me. I was now in the first grade and starting school in my hometown of 3500 people. When I had been in school a few weeks, my teacher called my mother and told her the school wanted to move me to the second grade because I already knew what was being taught in the first grade. Mother and Aunt Ann had taught me for the past two years at home and I was actually above the second-grade level. My mother said no, as she felt I needed to be with my own-age friends. My classmates were learning ABC's and numbers and learning to read *Dick and Jane* books. I already knew these things and owned the books that we were reading. I was bored to death when I had to participate in these drills about numbers and words. However, I made friends that have lasted for a lifetime so it was not a totally bad experience.

It is strange what lingers in a child's memory and what we choose not to forget. These are the most memorable parts of first grade in my hometown.

The first day of school, I stepped onto the dusty playground at the elementary school. I was dressed all in white, including white buckled shoes and socks. Actually, from the time I was born until the second day of school, my mother dressed me in all white. The only exception was when I played with the neighborhood boys and she let me wear shorts or pants and a shirt.

I could see my tomboy days were now limited. I was pleased that there were other girls on the playground. I'm sure with my fair complexion (due to being kept in the house so much until Mother was sure I was fully recovered from TB), my pale-blonde curly hair, and dressed in white, I was perceived to be an angelic, meek little girl.

I headed to the merry-go-round where only one little girl was riding. I later found out her name was Betty. I started pushing it faster to prepare to jump on when she said, "Get away, this is my merry-go-round." After making one more pass, I jumped on. She tried to push me off and said "You have to get off. I said nothing. All those past skirmishes with the neighborhood boys showed up that day, as I threw her off the merry-go-round. When she fell, she skinned her knee, began to cry and ran over to a teacher where she told on me. The teacher told me to get off the merry-go-round, and as it slowed down, I jumped off. The teacher said she was going to take us to the office. I had no idea what that meant so I was not concerned. Betty, however began to cry harder, so I was becoming a little concerned. This was my first trip to the principal's office where I met this stern, tall, plump woman with short white frizzy hair, named Miss Tanner.

Miss Tanner was very intimidating to all the students, with her size and height being part of the reason. When you are 6 years old and looking up, grown-ups look formidable. She made us both back up to the wall and tell our version of what had happened. Betty told her version which did not mention the part about it being her merry-go-round. Her nose was running because she had been crying and she looked pitiful. I was not crying yet. When it was my turn to tell the story, I told exactly the way it happened including my throwing her off. The whole time, Miss Tanner was holding a large paddle in her right hand, which she patted lightly on her right leg. It was bigger than any switch Mother had ever used on me and I was beginning to worry. However, once Miss Tanner had heard both stories, she said "Young ladies must share with each other and that includes everything on the playground. The playground belongs to all the students. If I see either of you come back to this office again, this paddle will be waiting. I will use it if you don't mind me." I believed her.

When the recesses came, I forgot I was a young lady and got so dirty in the white dress and ran so much, my socks slipped down into my shoes. We girls were all playing "tag," and the boys, including my neighborhood friends, had joined us. I had sweated, and the dust on the playground was all over my face and neck. The light-blonde hair was a lot sandier colored and matted as I had put my hands in it while I was playing. When Mother picked me up, the expression on her face told it all. She had never seen me any dirtier than I was that day. She took me to the department store in town and bought me colored clothes. That was my last day to wear white to school.

The second day of school at recess, I was on the monkey bars trying not to get in trouble, when I saw Miss Tanner coming toward me. I had been told by my mother not to climb up high on the monkey bars as my panties would show. I looked down to see if my panties were showing and no one was on the ground below me, so I knew she wasn't coming for me. I was trying to think what I might have done wrong this time, when she walked right past me and continued toward a tree on the edge of the property. There was a young woman sitting under the tree with her breast out and one of my classmates was cuddled in her lap nursing at her breast. I climbed up higher on the monkey bars to get a better view_totally oblivious to the panty problem. Almost all the other kids were watching too. I could hear Miss Tanner talking to the woman. She asked her why she was doing this and she told her the boy was hungry since he was used to being fed about this time. Miss Tanner said, "If he is old enough to come to school, he's too old to still be nursing. You need to go home or I'll have to call the police. I want to see him in class tomorrow and don't set foot on school property again except to drop him off and pick him up." The woman stood up and buttoned her blouse. Her son stood up and was clinging to her dress. She pulled him loose and started walking away. He cried when his mother left. Miss Tanner had him by the hand and he was still crying and looking back for his mother. Miss Tanner took him into the classroom without saying a word. The mother never returned and he was still attending when I finally transferred to the school where Aunt Ann lived.

Like all children who go to school, I'll never forget my first-grade teacher, Miss Corbin. This was her first year to teach. Several of the children ate white beans daily as part of their diet. This caused a lot of flatulence. Miss Corbin was determined to teach all of them not to "fart" in public. When the odor appeared, Miss Corbin would ask for a volunteer to smell each child's bottom until it was determined who was the villain.

Several hands would shoot up for the position of "smeller." It was always the boys' hands that were up. Whenever the perpetrator was caught, that person would have to walk to the window, and using their hand, fan their butts to chase the odor out of the room. This was supposed to embarrass them, I suppose. It certainly didn't help to get rid of the odor. It wasn't very effective, as the boys thought it was funny and the girls hated it. This didn't last long as some days we spent more time chasing stinkers than studying.

Some of the classmates from my all-white area were impoverished and many of them never wore shoes to school until it was cold outside. (Those shoes were provided by churches and families whose children had outgrown their shoes.) I was shocked at how one of my newfound playground friends lived, when my mother asked her to get in the car so we might take her home one day. Her name was Mary and no one ever picked her up. She didn't have a coat and it was a cold day.

They lived in the section of town that had houses with dirt floors. I had never seen this part of town before. These houses were old. The boards on the building had shrunk over time, and the people had used newspapers and magazines to fill the cracks and papered the walls to keep the cold out. The glue to hold the paper in place was often made from flour and water and attracted mice and rats that were hungry. All heat in this section was provided by a wood or coal stove. We knew Mary's house was heated with wood because of the color of her skin. If the source was coal for heat, it would leave an oily residue inside the house and on the occupants that was even blacker. You could always a tell a child who lived in these circumstances, as they looked as though they were darker skinned. They only bathed once a week for church, so you only saw the real color of their skin on Sundays in the winter. Summertime was hard as they had to sleep with doors and windows open. Few could afford screens so they slept under netting. Although my parents had started with a coal stove before I was born, they had converted to oil when I was 3. This experience made my home behind the grocery store heated with that oil stove seem elegant.

The other children in school were dressed nicely and were either local merchants' children, or those of farm owners. The wealthy farm families sent their children off to school up north or down south as soon as they finished eighth grade.

CHAPTER 29

CHANGE OF SCHOOLS

Aunt Ann told Mother and Daddy that they should be letting me move in with her and Uncle Billy as soon as school started. This would help end some of the stress showing on Mother. The town of 350 people Aunt Ann lived in was only eighteen miles from our town. Aunt Ann could not have children and she had been like a second mother to me since I was born. Nothing pleased me more than to go spend the night with her and my uncle. They fixed my favorite foods and played cards and games with me. My parents were always so busy they rarely had time to do these things. Mother and Daddy took Aunt Ann's offer into consideration, but declined as they were waiting in hopes that we could all be together.

A few months into the first grade, Mother could see that Aunt Ann was right. This was because Mother found out that many times when school was out in the afternoon, she would have a customer and she could not leave to come pick me up at school. It was too far for me to walk home and the school told her that I could no longer be left waiting as someone always had to stay with me. Mother asked a local soda shop owner named Powell, if I could walk to his place and she could pick me up there when she got finished at work. He and his wife said yes because, they, like everyone else in town, knew our circumstances. This worked for a while and I loved it. It was the teenage hangout. When I arrived there, they would tell me to go to a back booth, hand me a comic book to read and I'd order a snack and coke. I enjoyed watching the teenagers and seeing what they were wearing. Mother soon realized how often I was having to do this and what an imposition it was on the store owners. On her next visit to the sanatorium, she talked to Daddy and they made plans for me to move to the small town with Aunt Ann.

What a change it was for me. I just thought that my school had been boring as this small school's curriculum was behind my hometown's. During this period of time there was no such thing as kindergarten. Every child, unless they had been helped at home, was totally clueless when they stepped through education's door. I was reading on a fourth-grade level and already knew how to add and subtract. I had my hand up every time the teacher had a question, and I knew all the answers. This annoyed the teacher enough that she called Aunt Ann. Having taught eight grades in school like my mother, Aunt Ann proposed that the teacher let me help her teach the students to read. This was a great help to all and made me feel important. A new school and a new life began.

Uncle Billy and Aunt Ann always made me a peanut-butter-and-jelly sandwich to take to school. Peanut butter was not blended with corn syrup then and the oil would sit on top of the pureed peanuts. The moment you opened the jar, the odor was pure oil and nauseating. You had to use a large spoon, stirring hard and fast to blend the peanut butter and oil together. Once it was blended, you had to spread it on the peanut butter sandwich quickly before the oil separated again. I hated peanut butter. I didn't want to tell Aunt Ann and Uncle Billy that I didn't like it, because I was afraid I'd hurt their feelings. I would throw the sandwich away and drink the milk that was provided for lunch. By the end of the school day, I was famished.

Aunt Ann had been appointed to the postmaster position in this small town by Harry Truman, who was a Senator at the time. When she got the telegram from Senator Truman saying she had been selected, she was surprised and so was her husband, Uncle Billy. A woman postmaster was a rarity. She had started her career working when she had gotten out of college as a schoolteacher in a rural area. When the war began, Aunt Ann quit teaching and took a job working for the government, teaching women how to grow vegetable and fruit gardens. She then would teach them how to can the produce they had grown. After having this job, she saw what benefits were to be had working for the government. She started looking for something else in that field. The postmaster position became available and although she submitted her resume, she did not expect to be the one selected.

After school, I would have to go to the post office until Aunt Ann finished work at five, and I was with her from 4:45 p.m. to 5:00 p.m. Government regulations said unless you were a post office employee, you could not be in the private part of the post office. There was nothing Aunt Ann could do with me except try to hide me from the public. Uncle Billy was a farmer and had to take off from work to pick me up at school, so he couldn't take me back to the farm with him. Since the post office boxes covered most of the small building and you could see through them into the back, that left a very small spot for me to hide in. I had to sit on the floor behind a desk with the outgoing mailbags stacked in front of me. I would spend that time reading or coloring for the remaining hour and a half.

At that time all the postage was hand-stamped with the town name and date of mailing. There were no zip codes, and most of the mail that was not placed in the boxes had to be delivered by foot in the small town. The postmaster did every job and only had one helper. If the mail delivery came at night, she would have to go to the post office to let the mail truck in to receive the new mail. At that time, she would give the delivery man the outgoing mailbags that were my secret hide-away. If the weather was bad and he was late, he would come to her house and honk. She would then meet him at the post office. She also had to fill out numerous reports, mainly financial, regarding postage sales. Because she was ambidextrous, she could fill out two reports at the same time. There was no such thing as a photocopier, and often they would use carbon paper to make the copy. Unless you pressed really hard with your pen, the copy might not be legible. I can't say her penmanship was that great, but writing with both hands at the same time, certainly helped to get things done quicker and impressed me!

There was not much entertainment in this small town where Aunt Ann lived. No movie theater, so a local gas station would clean up its shop on Sundays and set up folding chairs and a movie screen, to show whatever movie they could afford to buy. I saw the original *King Kong*—which had already been out for seventeen years——while eating popcorn out of a brown paper sack and drinking a Coca Cola - out of a bottle. The smell of gas and oil floated in the room. It was hot and stuffy because the doors had to be closed to make it dark enough for the movie screen. No air could come in the windows as they were covered with drop cloths. A big shop fan blew constantly, sometimes drowning out the sound from the screen in an effort to cool off the audience. All of this for 25 cents!

I played cards with my aunt and uncle two or three times a week and read books for entertainment. There were some of my cousins to play with on the weekends, so I was not bored. Uncle Billy and Aunt Ann played canasta with their friends in the evening on weekends, so I had to find some way to entertain myself. Aunt Ann had taught me to embroider, so I would sit in the background and work on this colorful hobby while listening to the different conversations of the adults.

Aunt Ann was perfect for this small town. She had made lots of friends as she loved to socialize and was very active in the church. Aunt Ann, as a postmaster was loved in the community by both blacks and whites. She loved them all in return. She helped all her customers who were unable to fill out papers and would read mail from relatives to those who were illiterate. She also helped compose letters for those they could not write. She thought it was important that everyone be able to write their names instead of using an "X." She loved to see the joy on the face of someone who had mastered this simple task. Everyone called her Miss Ann and the government was so pleased with her that she retained this job for thirty-five years.

CHAPTER 30

THE COMPANY STORE

The post office was located in a building shared with a "company store" named Petersons. The Peterson family owned large amounts of farmland, cotton bins and grain storage tanks. Most of the farming was done by hand, hoeing cotton, corn and soybeans as well as chopping and picking cotton. There were hundreds of people who worked on these company store farms and they were not paid a salary. The owners provided a home for each family, and everything they wanted or needed came from the company store. An account was kept of their purchases of food and clothing all year. When the crops came in, they would come to the store and "settle up." If there was any extra money due them that had not been spent at the store, that money was paid to them at harvest time. Many farmhands, who had now been paid out, would then take their provisions in large quantities for the following crop year. This saved buying it all year in smaller parcels, plus making the trip to town to get it (fifty-gallon barrels of flour and cornmeal would be a typical example). The store was a general store so it also was available to the public.

Some of the company stores started a game for the farmhands which involved filling up a wooden barrel with dollar bills. It was just a little extra something to give the employees as a bonus at the end of the year. They made a hole in the barrel, about the size of a hand, that every worker was allowed to put his hand through. He would then try to pull out as many one-dollar bills as he could grab. He only had one chance. They would line up and take turns, and there would be much encouragement and laughing as each one tried to get the most. There was never a lot pulled out as it is hard to make a fist and pull it out of a small hole when your hand is full. Regardless, they all looked forward to doing it as it had become a source of entertainment and also a tradition.

This small town where Aunt Ann worked was segregated by a railroad track, with the blacks living across the tracks from the town. Most of the people living there had jobs in the small town other than farming. Most of the houses were "shotgun houses" which were composed of three rooms. Upon entering the front door was the living area, second room was the bedroom, and the third room was usually the kitchen. They all had outdoor toilets. They called these houses shotguns, because if you should fire a shot at the front door, it would go clean through the house and out the back door, never hitting a thing inside.

CHAPTER 31

AUNT ANN AND UNCLE BILLY

Aunt Ann had been married a long time and was unable to have children. She doted on me. She taught me everything that made me feel good about myself, and she played a big part in raising me up to the age of 7. This was due, as mentioned, to health problems that kept my father in and out of hospitals. Aunt Ann knew that Mother was not able to run the business by herself, and take care of both my father and me at the same time. She was always available when Mother needed her.

Aunt Ann's husband, uncle Billy, was wonderful to me. When he was not farming, he would let me sleep as long as I wanted. When I got up, he would have large biscuits that he called "cat-heads," baked for my breakfast along with chocolate milk. Every day when he returned from work, he would put all his pennies in a drawer. He had started this habit when I was born. When he had enough pennies to buy a Savings Bond, he would have me help him roll them up in coin containers. Then he would purchase a twenty-five-dollar savings bond in my name. His plan was to give me this money when I was old enough for college.

Aunt Ann was a member of the Methodist Church and took me every week to Sunday school and church. Sunday school was very entertaining as I always enjoyed the Bible stories. The only annoying thing about this class was a blonde-haired girl named Mary Lou, who, as soon as I sat down in Sunday school, wanted to hold my purse. She then opened it up and browsed through it until the class was over. Some Sundays, it was someone else's purse she would select. No one ever complained, but I'm sure they were as irritated by this as I was.

The third time she grabbed my purse as I was walking in the door. Her hand was not going to find much, because there was nothing inside except my handkerchief (that my aunt insisted I carry), my package of Juicy Fruit gum which Mary Lou always opened and chewed, and some tokens from the local store that I was hoping to redeem for candy. But today she blew her nose on my handkerchief, that my aunt had embroidered the little black Scottie dog on. That did it; I decided she'd held my purse for the last time! I jumped up and walked over to her while the teacher was talking about David and Goliath. I grabbed the purse and told her never to hold it again. She told me that I was selfish and God was going to punish me.

At that point, the teacher stopped in the middle of her Bible story, just as David had confronted Goliath, and I expected her to say something to us. She did not. Everyone was looking at us. I told Mary Lou that if she wanted a purse to hold, she should ask her mom for one instead of holding everyone else's purse. She said she was not going to be my friend anymore. I was speechless, because this was the first time I had even realized that she thought we were friends. My silence was broken by the teacher continuing to read about David as though nothing had happened. The teacher was the only one interested in what became of Goliath as everyone else was watching to see what was going to happen with Mary Lou and me. Mary Lou sat down with her bottom lip pooched out, and I sat down with a frown and my purse.

Why the Sunday-school teacher never seemed to notice this

annoying girl's continued purse fixation, was strange to me. Later I found out: the teacher was her aunt.

After Sunday school, we joined the adults for church. I was as bored as a child can be when the sermon was delivered, so I would spend my time counting how many hats were in the room, how many people had on black, etc. I did pay attention when they began to sing the hymn because I always enjoyed singing. I loved to go with Aunt Ann on those Sundays because we would dress up and she would fix my hair. None of these things had been experienced at home, as my mother and father never went to church, so it was a rare occasion that required me to dress up. Aunt Ann also taught me to memorize the Lord's Prayer and how to say grace at meals. Church was a pleasant experience that has lasted my lifetime.

After a few months of school, it appeared that I was making no progress, but merely repeating what I already knew. Aunt Ann and Uncle Billy decided to drive me back the eighteen miles to my original school to finish first grade. He would then pick me up after school. Next fall, I was placed in a class that was being taught both second and third grade because of a lack of teachers. It was decided that since I was more advanced, I could participate in part of the third-grade curriculum, and the rest in the second-grade studies. This trip back and forth was a hardship on Uncle Billy because he needed to be in the fields. Mother could not help him because this was also her busiest time of year.

CHAPTER 32

THE PIANO PLAYER

May 1950

My daddy could play the piano, violin and guitar "by ear" and wanted me to excel at music. Mother and he decided when I was 6 to forego buying a car that they really needed, in order to purchase an upright piano. Ideally, I would take piano lessons and Daddy would play the piano when he felt like it. He was hopeful that I had inherited his ability to play by ear and would not really need the lessons. As we later found out, that did not happen.

I remember the day the large truck pulled up behind our grocery store to unload the piano. The neighbors came to watch, as in this small town, any event—no matter how small—was expected to be shared with all the neighbors.

The delivery men were in a quandary as to how they were going to fit the piano into the small living room. There was the matter of the coal stove in the middle, along with a sofa and two chairs. They took out one chair and placed the piano against the wall. About 6 inches of the piano covered the door into the bedroom. One of the technicians tuned the piano. The neighbors were all standing on the porch looking through the windows and the doorway. They stayed to listen to the tedious job of tuning the piano.

One man in particular was more excited than we were about our new purchase. His name was Henry Mayberry. He had fought in World War II and had been injured, which required a metal plate to be put inside his skull. This was not an uncommon situation as several Vets had experienced this. It often changed their ability to work as well as socialize. Henry wandered around town all day, stopping to visit at the businesses or anyone in their yard or on their porch. He smoked cigarettes continually. This was a habit he had picked up in the war when the cigarette companies sent free cigarettes to the warfront. When he saw the delivery truck and the gathering, he worked his way to the front to see what was happening. His eyes lit up when he saw the piano being unloaded and he appeared to be very nervous. Henry had sometimes played the piano in the tavern that my parents had owned before he went to war.

He had not been able to find a piano to play since his return from the hospital after the war. The minute the delivery men closed up their truck and pulled away, Henry opened our screen door and walked in. He sat down at the piano and began to play. His style of music was best described as "honky-tonk." He played for over an hour with some of the observers still listening from the porch. Finally, he played a song called, "Goodnight Irene, Goodnight" then stood up without a word, and walked out the door. We all applauded as he left, as happy for his leaving as we were for the concert. My parents told me that he always played the "Goodnight" song at the tavern to alert the customers that they were closing.

Unfortunately, the newfound piano became a weekly visit for Henry. My parents were too kind to ask him to leave and were anxious to hear "Goodnight" be played every time he visited. Mother finally decided to try a new technique to get Henry to shorten his playing. The next time, after he had played two songs,

Mother requested "Goodnight." He played it, got up then left, totally unaware that his "concert" had been shortened. All this was fine until several months later when Henry smoked a cigarette and, while playing, an ash fell, landing on the keyboard where it burned a hole in one of the ivories. Mother asked him to leave before "Goodnight." After that, they locked the door and refused to let him back in.

Now that Henry was not coming on a regular basis, Daddy was ready to attempt to teach me how to play melodies that I heard him play. After several failed attempts, my lessons were scheduled to begin as I definitely could not play by ear.

CHAPTER 33

MISS BEATRICE

My piano teacher was named Miss Beatrice. She was a 60-year-old, short woman who was described as stout. Her clothing was always very colorful with large flowers, but she had a black shawl with a fringe that she kept wrapped around her in the cool weather. I had asked my mother one time if she was a Gypsy. She said, "No one knows, maybe she is just different." She had salt-and-pepper-colored hair that she always tied up in a bun. It always had several strands of hair that wriggled their way out to hang down above her eyes. When I was practicing, she would be sitting on the bench with me, keeping time by counting and simultaneously blowing those strands out of her face.

She always wore hose with garters holding them up. The top of the hose was rolled up in the garters. By the time late afternoon came, the garters were slipping down, allowing the hose to become lose and wrinkled around her ankles. Hose during that time had a seam up the back that you were supposed to keep straight as a stick. Her seams looked more like a worm attempting to crawl down in her black lace-up shoes that were the type older women wore. She wore glasses which, perched on the end of her nose, made her hold her head back. Otherwise, they would have slid down the end of her nose. Sometimes when it was hot, her face had perspiration on it. She would stop to fan herself and say "Hot flashes" then put the glasses aside, move her face closer to the music and squint at what I was attempting to play.

Her telephone sat across from the piano. When it would ring, she would jump up to answer it. Once the receiver was in her hand, she would say loudly, "Start talking!" Once the short conversation was over with, she would hang up without acknowledging the person on the other end with a goodbye. In all the seven years she taught me, I never heard her say hello or goodbye. She used a cigarette holder to dial the phone, but I don't think she ever smoked. When it was miserably hot, she had a fan which sometimes blew the sheet music off the music rack. To hold it in place, she would take hair pins out of her hair and attach the music to a heavier music book behind it.

Her house was an old home but looked like what you could currently call Bohemian-style clutter. She had music stacked up all over the floor and on a built-in bench by the window. In the second room, she had an organ, a set of drums, racks to hold violins and several racks of accordions. The accordions were positioned so that she might teach three students at the same time. Accordions were all the rage as Lawrence Welk was at the peak of his career. Everyone wanted to play the accordion, except me.

She had a small kitchen with a dinky refrigerator. She rarely put anything away after she used it so the counters were covered with dishes, condiments, spices, etc. She had all kinds of store-bought medications sitting around the room for indigestion and various other ailments.

For some reason, she selected me to be her errand runner. When Mother would drop me off for the lesson, she would leave the room where the student before me was taking their lesson, to talk to me. She would give me some money then have me walk to the grocery store to buy her one slice of salami. Sometimes, I would also be asked to pick up a loaf of bread. When I returned, she would be finished with the prior student. She would be sitting at the piano playing and singing her favorite song, "Bye Bye Blackbird." After she had finished the song then put away the salami, she would start my lesson. My hour lesson was always more like a half-hour lesson because of the trip to town and the entertainment she provided prior to starting.

I was suspicious that Daddy had encouraged her to teach me "chording" since he played by ear, because several times she would give me a piece of music to play then mark the bass with chords, instead of using the music notes provided. That didn't work; I still couldn't do it. She quit after the second year of trying and let me play what was on the sheet music.

Once home from school, daily, my mother would have me practice piano for thirty minutes before I was allowed to play, do homework or read. My parents wanted to know if there was some other instrument that I might perform on better than the piano since I was not progressing as fast as they had hoped. Miss Beatrice suggested starting organ lessons, which was a mediocre experience, followed by accordion lessons which was a dismal failure, and, finally, the violin—very humdrum. They refused to let me take drum lessons, thank goodness. I finally became better at the piano. I didn't appreciate how grateful I would be for these piano lessons until I was a grown woman. All those years of practice helped me be proficient enough to entertain my family and myself.

CHAPTER 34

1950, MOVING TO THE FARM

In 1950, I turned 7 when Daddy was released from the hospital after a six-month stay. He had been unable to continue his alcohol addiction while there because of the seclusion. Mother and I were hopeful that this would mean an end to his drinking. But not long after he returned home, he started again. It seemed his dry spell had caused him to accelerate the amount he was now drinking daily. I realized this in his actions that sometimes placed us in harm's way.

That year, they purchased a 120-acre farm, complete with a three-bedroom, two-story farmhouse, two barns, a smokehouse to cure meat, a chicken house, wash house and an outhouse with one hole. This also included the first bedroom that I did not have to share with my mother. The farm equipment business was good, so we remodeled the house! We had no use for the smokehouse so it was torn down. We added a full bathroom indoors but kept the outhouse for emergencies. The protocol for using the outhouse was to keep an old Sears catalog by the hole. You would use the sheets for toilet paper. First when you entered the outhouse, you would grab a few sheets of the catalog then set them on fire with a match. You would then wave the paper torch around inside the toilet hole to clear out spiders and other bugs. This was very important as black widow spiders, who are poisonous, were known to make their nests there. Some people had sat down and been bitten in very delicate places. Once this ritual was performed you could go on with your business. If you truly had an emergency, you might as well have stayed in the house where the ritual was not needed.

The wash house had a shower in it and the room was warmed by a small wood-burning stove. We had a separate area where we washed clothes in a new wringer washer. No more hauling hot water and making your fingers bloody on the rub board. We would wash the clothes and put them through the wringer to fall into a raised wash tub filled with rinse water. Then we'd run it back through the wringer. Next, we'd hang it out on a clothesline to dry. For our white clothes, we would use another tub of cold water with a product called "bluing" that would make the white clothes bright white. This sounds like lots of work, but it was a large step up from pumping the water, heating and hauling it to put in a tub, and scrubbing every piece on a rub board.

Our chicken house had twelve chickens—ten hens and two roosters. We always had chicken for supper on Sundays. Mother would grab a random chicken by the neck and wring the neck until the head came off. Then the chicken would run around the yard sporadically until it died. If you ever heard the expression," I was running around like a chicken with its head off" this was what was being referenced. Then she would hang it up by its feet and drain the blood. Next would come a container of boiling water to soften up the feathers so you could pull them out easily. The odor of these wet feathers in the water was disgusting. I always was asked to help pull the feathers. Not a pleasant thing. Then mother made sure all the "pin feathers" were gone. If not, she would light a piece of newspaper with a match to burn them off. Lastly, you washed the chicken, cut it up, and it was ready to be fried for supper.

Our chickens were definitely "free range" chickens. When I hear that someone has requested a free-range chicken, I always wonder why. Free-range chickens poop in the yard and come back later to eat their own feces. As cruel as contained chicken houses seem to be, the chickens can't get to the feces. it has to be a lot more sanitary, where they don't move around freely, and eat nutritional food only.

When we moved onto the farm, Daddy began to change it. The previous owners had run cattle and had a large concrete scale where they weighed cattle and grain trucks. Daddy decided to sell the cattle. He also wanted to use dynamite to blast the concrete scales out of the ground so he could start his row-crop production instead.

He studied a book about how to use the dynamite and assured Mother that the blast was far enough away from the house (which had just been renovated) that it would not harm it. Daddy had adhered to the county sheriff's department rules for use of dynamite. He had gotten permission for the use of the dynamite. The sheriff had blocked off the highway in both directions since the scales were not far from the highway. Everything seemed to be adequately prepared for the event. A lot of neighbors were watching from a safe distance as the preparation began. No one knew it, but Daddy had decided to add a little more dynamite than the instructions called for in his instruction book. He was very sober that morning so all of us felt pretty secure about the scale removal.

My mother and I were in the house when he set off the charge. It shook the surroundings so violently that both of the large barns moved and the ground felt like an earthquake! The concrete blew into so many small pieces that they reached the house. They broke some of the new windows and made permanent pock marks in the wood siding.

When Mother and I saw the concrete flying toward us, we moved quickly to an inside room. That move was just in time, as we heard the window breakage and multiple blows against the house. It took days to clean up the concrete as it had made a perfect circle of debris around the scales. Every piece had to be picked up from the field in order to farm it. The highway department was busy cleaning off the road in front of the house so traffic could flow through. If Daddy was sober when he did this, I shudder to think what we would have experienced had he been drinking. Daddy was not charged for the damage as they never discovered if he had meant to use the larger amount or if it was an accidental miscalculation.

Now the scales were gone and the holes had been filled where the scales had been. The cattle had been sold. Our crop rotation would start immediately that fall. Our first crop was alfalfa which could be cut, at thirty-five-day intervals until the fall, as it would regrow numerous times. Daddy would plant it after the last frost in the spring and before the first frost in the fall. We would send it to an alfalfa mill nearby to be processed. Our other crop which we rotated was cotton. It was a physical-labor crop.

A large group of black people would come to chop and pick our cotton. Our farm was divided from the small town by a county road. No black person would step foot into the town because they were afraid of violence. The town had a reputation of being rough not only to the "colored" but to anyone that was a stranger. Black people were allowed in town to shop one day a week and they had to be out of the town by sunset.

CHAPTER 35

1951, CHURCH

When I was returned to my home, I was still in second grade. We were still taking the long trip to visit Daddy. I thought this would be a good time to ask them to take me to the Methodist church in Weston or the Apostles of God that my dad's family attended. Mother's response was she did not believe in God, but Daddy said he read the Bible every day. He said he felt no need for "structured religious training." He did indeed read the Bible every day, wearing out two Bibles in his lifetime. He had a strong belief in God but was not willing to share that belief in church with other believers.

My grandparents on both sides were upset that I could not attend church. My dad's father, Calvin, had been a part-time minister when they lived on the island. He was a very generous contributor for the funding of the Apostles Church. He believed that you should only keep as much of your income as you needed for survival while the rest should be given to the church. If you kept a profit, it was a sin in his mind. My dad did not share his father's strict beliefs. I knew there was no way he could talk Daddy into saying he would attend with me. My mother's mom, Clarissa Clay, was a Methodist, so she had encouraged Mother to

145

take me to her church. My parents were receiving pressure from both sides.

Since Daddy was still in the hospital, Mother's decision to appease the grandparents was to dress me up on Sunday then drop me at the Methodist Church door. If she left me alone at the church, I think she thought this would deter me, as a small child wouldn't want to attend alone. It didn't. The first time she took me to the church I was apprehensive but knew if I didn't go inside, I would not be offered the opportunity again. She pulled up to the curb to let me out. I opened the door and stepped out of the car and Mother said, "I will pick you up in this spot when church is over." People were beginning to file in the door as I ascended the steps. Most of them knew me and were neighbors or friends. They watched Mother drive off. If they found it strange that I was alone, they never said. I walked inside with the others.

I already knew what Sunday school was, so I asked the man standing inside the door where the Sunday school class was located. He walked me to it and introduced me to the teacher, Mr. Worth. He was a very friendly man and knew how to keep children interested in religion. He played games to help you learn about the Bible. One of the games was to learn all the books of the Bible. If you could recite the Old and New Testaments all in order, he would give you a colorful lockbox with a key. I wanted the box, so I went home determined to learn to recite all the books of the Bible. It took me a month before I was ready to recite them in front of the class. I couldn't pronounce all the biblical names correctly, but it was close enough for me to win. He also took us on a field trip once a month. The field trips were skating rinks, swimming pools and movies. His class was large and everyone was very competitive. The age group was 6 through 9 years of age.

When Sunday school was over the first day I attended, I looked outside for my mother but her car was not in sight. I then realized that I had to stay for church. I sat down in the last row on the aisle. All the people stared at me, so I picked up a song-book and looked at the pages. When I walked outside after church, Mother was waiting. She said, "How was church?" I said "Great, but when they passed the basket, I did not have any money." She said she would send some with me if I decided to go again.

This began my peculiar religious upbringing. I went every week. My Methodist grandmother, Clarissa Clay (who lived in California every winter), was very pleased I was attending, but my Grandfather Constantine, on my daddy's side, wanted me at his church. Of all people to resolve the problem of where I should go, I least expected Mother to find a solution. She did have a unique idea to please both families.

CHAPTER 36

CAMP MEETING

Grandfather Constantine's church, The Apostles of God, had a program in the summer called a "camp meeting" that was a week in duration. This was an outdoor affair in tents where they would have programs, games and music for the children that was repeated daily. During the day, there was also Bible school for children plus Bible study for ladies.

Lunch was served potluck every day, offering sandwiches, casseroles and desserts. The evening meal was frequently fried catfish, hush puppies and coleslaw, followed by dessert. All the fish was cooked in the open on campfires in large, black iron kettles. Not only did people from the Apostle church attend, but all denominations and non-Christians came nightly to hear a visiting Evangelist preach as well as hear the Gospel music. Some of the Gospel singers who performed would later become famous. There was also a "his and hers outhouse" they had built on the outside perimeter in order to keep people from going home to the bathroom as they might not come back.

Grandmother Clay had become a five-foot-seven, 200-pound woman with very strict rules. She was home for the summer, keeping all of her grandchildren in line. Raising seven children by herself had probably made her strict. I called her "Big Momma." She would join "Little Momma" and me nightly at the camp meeting. I soon learned where my parents got their ideas for raising children. I learned a lot sitting between Grandmother Constantine and Grandmother Clay.

Later that summer, the camp meeting was in full swing. I was attending with both my grandmothers. I had always called Maeve, Little Momma. She spoiled me and allowed me to move around in my seat and be a general nuisance to others who were trying to listen. My parents had a rule that when we went anywhere, I was to sit still between them but never say a word unless I was spoken to. Then my response was always yes or no, ma'am, and yes or no, sir. Because of her patience, kindness, and letting me have my way, Little Momma was a delight to be with and I loved her.

Every time I would squirm in my seat, Big Momma would pinch me and I would cry. At this same action, Little Momma would put her arm around me to love me. I soon became more aware of what the preacher's message was since I had no choice but to listen. I still loved Big Momma.

The Apostles had erected a permanent structure with no walls where visiting preachers would come in the evenings to deliver their message. The structure was directly behind the church. Gospel quartets would sing all the wonderful old songs like "I'll Fly Away" and "The Blood of the Lamb." The end of the evening preaching would conclude with the song, "Jesus is Calling," and due to the fervor of the preacher's "Hell and Damnation" sermon," would-be converts would hasten down the aisle to be converted to Christianity. Present church members would also come down to be forgiven for their sins and recommit themselves to the Lord. Most of the people would be very emotional, crying or praising the Lord with every breath. I was very moved by these converts and, until this day, I treasure this part of my upbringing. Once converted, the followers would all be baptized in the river or a local ditch, following the conclusion of the camp meeting. Otherwise, the church had a large pool behind the altar that would be used for their Baptism at a selected time.

Camp meeting was hot and humid. All the ladies were always dressed up in their cotton, flower-print dresses. Most wore a fancy hat. They would be clutching a paper fan advertising the local funeral home. These fans were used to stir up the hot breezes plus ward off the mosquitoes. The men were always in suits and ties. In those days, any man who was anyone wore a hat. The men's hats were always promptly removed when they entered the tent building to show respect.

Although the campground had been sprayed for mosquitoes with DDT, you still had to battle the mosquitoes off of you from time to time. If there had been a rain, I suppose it would wash away the spray that had been used to combat them. The women were more vulnerable to the bites because they were in dresses with their legs and arms exposed. The men would take off their suit jackets and still have on a long-sleeved shirt which helped protect them. I was there for the whole program. Seven days of Christian atmosphere! I loved it and attended every year until I was in my teens.

CHAPTER 37

1951-52, PLAYMATES

This part of my life was pretty average. The only difference was Daddy had started drinking again. He was starting earlier every morning and was finished with a fifth of bourbon by night. I tried to be like Mother, who acted like nothing was different at our house. The neighborhood was full of boys. No girlfriends available, except at school. I played boy games with them every day. I was always picked last for baseball because I was a girl, but they needed me to make a team. One of the boys, Robert, was a bully who used to fight me every once in a while. I could not win as he was bigger than me, so I would beat on his little brother, Chuckie. I soon realized that was silly so I quit picking on Chuckie. Will was the other boy in the neighborhood. He was my favorite. He didn't care if I was a girl, always treating me like an equal. We all played marbles together a lot. We would lose marbles to each other then win them back in the next few days.

Another friend, Bobby, was an only child and his mother called him Baby Boy. He was not allowed to play with us much, because he was afraid of Robert and his mother knew it. One day, he brought his marbles then said he wanted to play with the rest of us. He picked me to play against him since he was afraid of

Robert. He lost all his marbles to me. He asked for his marbles back but I said no and the boys laughed. He picked up the empty sack then ran home. He must have told his mother about losing his marbles to me. She and Billy came to our house and his face was red from crying. His mother told my parents she wanted Bobby's marbles back. My parents said that would be fine so I gave them back. I never played marbles with him again. Daddy had watched me give the marbles back. He told me Bobby was a sore loser and was aptly named by his mother. I didn't know what "aptly named" meant until I was older.

Once, the boys and I were playing cowboys and Indians. We had a post we had found in the barnyard behind the house. The boys brought a shovel to set the post up in our side yard. The day before, we had been down to the edge of a ditch to cut bamboo cane to make a bows and arrows. We had also picked up several feathers from a dead hawk we had found. Some of the feathers were on the bamboo arrows while the bigger feathers were in our hair. Robert said we needed to have something to tie to the post for a prisoner. I ran in the house and got a doll that had been given to me for Christmas that I had named Brenda. I never enjoyed playing with dolls as I had no girlfriends to teach me how to play house or momma. I had never been around a baby and Mother never was interested in teaching me what to do with a doll. Brenda had a composition face but legs and arms that were made of a rubber composite.

Robert took some kite string then tied Brenda to the pole. Robert said, "We are going to burn her at the stake." I was a little apprehensive about this, but I had volunteered Brenda plus I did not know that Robert had a match. I still though we were playing "pretend." The boys gathered sticks then set them on fire at the base of the pole. We then began a "war dance" around the pole. As the fire reached higher, Brenda began to slide down the pole and her dress was in danger of catching fire as the heat was getting closer to her legs! About that time, my mother had heard the war dance chants, then looked outside to see what was happening in the yard. She came running out the door with a bucket of water to douse the fire. She didn't make it before Brenda's legs and arms began to change color. Brenda was taken off the pole, promptly. Mother had the doll by one hand and was dragging me in the house by the other hand. She was yelling at the boys to go home and told them she would be over to see their mothers.

I was paddled as soon as Mother finished lecturing me about the dangers of playing with fire. Then, true to her word, she left to go tattle on the boys. They all received a paddling, too. When she returned, I was sent to my room and she told me I would never be given another doll. That was the least troubling thing she did, because I really didn't care about the doll. I never received another doll. I must have had a guilt complex about it that I didn't realize, as I still have Brenda. Her legs and arms are still black, but her head still has the painted brown hair. Her face has a sweet smile with the rosy cheeks and big eyes with long lashes.

I was always a daredevil. The three boys who were my usual playmates of the neighborhood had trapped a steer in a loading chute behind my father's farm equipment business. This area had always been a large field that I used for a shortcut to school. Someone had purchased it and turned it into a small livestock farm. The boys were taking turns climbing over the sides of the chute then dropping onto the steer's back. Of course, they were immediately thrown off. I was the only one who hadn't done it. They said I was a "sissy" and afraid. They "double-dog dared me" to get on the steer. So, I climbed the side of the chute then jumped on, not realizing that I really was a sissy in some things, being a girl. The steer arched his back, took one leap, and I was thrown off right over the chute. When I hit the ground, it knocked the breath out of me. I couldn't talk or get up so I lay flat on my back trying to breathe. One of the boys thought I was dying or dead. He told the others to run, so they all ran off and left me. I soon got up and walked home, sore but a lot wiser.

CHAPTER 38

PICKING COTTON

Segregation was still in effect in the United States, but my dad paid no attention to it. He always said that everyone on earth was just trying to live out this life as good as they could. I was always allowed to play with the black children who came along with their parents to work on the farm. Only-children always enjoy another child their own age. What color they were was not a factor.

I wanted to pick cotton so I could make some money like some of the other kids were doing. I was too small to tote one of the large white, cotton canvas sacks used by the other workers. So, Mother took a burlap sack and sewed a strap on it. It was less than half the length of the white sacks. My purpose for picking was to save enough money for the carnival rides which came to town, after the cotton harvest. That would be the last time I would pick cotton until the following year. Other times, I would pick just to make enough money to go to the local movie theater. When I reached my money goal, I would quit. The adults that were picking were dragging the long white bags down the rows, striving to pick a hundred pounds a day, which was hard to obtain. They were all very competitive with each other and visited and sang as they worked.

The cotton wagon had a weight scale on it where you weighed your pickings. One day when I was picking, one of the kids told me that if I would put a rock or a dirt clod in the bottom of the sack it would weigh more and I could make my money quicker. I did it, and of course I got caught and the kids all laughed. Their parents and my daddy weren't laughing. My dad told me I was setting a bad example for his employees, and his being angry with me hurt me more than a paddling. The best part of the cotton experience was playing in the cotton wagon with the other kids. We would jump off the sides into the cotton and roll around making the cotton more compact. We thought that we were doing a good thing, as we were making more room for the cotton in the wagon, which meant fewer trips to the cotton gin.

Once I had my carnival money from picking cotton, I would be watching for the carnival crew to set up the rides. I could climb up in our big barn and watch it all being put together. The carnival rides were within walking distance of my house. I would meet my school friends and ride every ride. The wilder the ride, the more we liked it. The next day, with all my money spent, I would be back picking cotton.

CHAPTER 39

STRANGE FRIENDSHIP DEVELOPS

This year was the beginning of a peculiar friendship. Daddy became best buddies with his previous tractor dealership competitor, T.J. Denton. His business was two doors down from ours and across a county road from our farm home. Daddy would walk home from work and stop at TJ's to share liquor every day. TJ had given up his farm equipment sales to start a new venture, so he was no longer in competition with Daddy. He became an entrepreneur who made several fortunes with inventions. He manufactured these products and became very wealthy. He had lots of employees he could not keep, due to his excessive drinking which caused him to be mean to them. He always carried a revolver inside his suit-coat jacket. Sometimes he would walk into the shop where the employees were, brandishing the gun and threatening to shoot it when he was upset over some small problem. He was always drunk when this happened and some employees were afraid of being shot. It was hard to build a good relationship with an employee who feared you.

Daddy had no fear of TJ. He would start drinking with him when he closed his business around five every evening. This would continue until it was nearly dark. Then he would walk the short distance from TJ's business to the ditch, jump over, cross the county road, jump the second ditch, and he would be on our homestead. Some days, Daddy drank so much that he couldn't jump the ditch. A few times he fell in it and crawled out. Unable to stand, he ended up crossing the road and the next ditch on his hands and knees. This embarrassed Mother, but there was nothing she could do about it. My bedroom faced the county road. I had watched him come across the road when cars would be going back and forth on the highway in front of the house. I just hoped no one would turn onto the county road and run over him. Due to his good luck, they did not.

TJ loved to flaunt his money by buying expensive cars and lots of nice, extravagant clothing. He had a beautiful second wife named Selena who benefited from this newfound wealth. Often when TJ was drunk, he would call his wife, different politicians, as well as local people to cuss them out over the phone. If they hung up, he would think there was something wrong with his phone. It never occurred to him that people did not want to be cussed out. Their hanging up would upset him so badly, that he would yank the phone cord out of the wall. After several of these episodes, the phone company refused to let him have any more service. Lost employees and inability to receive orders for his product over the phone caused him to go bankrupt. This did not deter him as he started a new company with a new name, two more times in the course of ten years. He repeated the same bad habits and lack of proper management each time. He made and lost two more fortunes.

During the duration of his second business, TJ had acquired a new group of friends. They were mainly a bunch of guys he had been furnishing free liquor to at one of the local bars. One of these friends who was an avid hunter suggested TJ should buy a shotgun and go duck hunting with them. TJ had never hunted, having only owned a revolver. The friend gave him a list of things he should purchase to be a successful hunter. On the list of items, he would need duck decoys. He was drunk the day he ordered the decoys. He called a wholesale company who sold them. The salesperson told him that using more decoys attracted more ducks. When he asked how many decoys TJ wanted, he answered "a truckload." They did not question the large order as he was calling from a manufacturing facility. TJ sent his largest truck to pick up the decoys and the salesperson made sure that it was filled up. When they delivered this large quantity, TJ had to build two buildings to house them all. The overflow of decoys was left in the buildings behind the manufacturing plant. When we had big rains, many of the decoys would float down the ditch. He now had everything he needed to hunt, except he had lost the friendship of the hunter who encouraged these purchases.

A family of children had just recently moved into a house behind TJ's buildings. They picked the decoys up and tied several together with a string and played with them in the ditches. Some hunters would see them floating down the ditch and pick them up to use for their hunting expeditions. I don't think TJ ever went hunting and used those dummy ducks. The decoys remained in the buildings and yard until TJ went broke for the last time.

Around the time of his second business failure, things were not going well with his marriage. His wife, Selena, and he had a terrible fight where he ended up pulling some of her long black hair out. She went to the beauty shop next day. Once there, she told the beauty operator she wanted her head shaved, because TJ hated short hair. She put all the shaven hair in a sack then took it home. When TJ came home that night, he was furious when he saw her shaven head. She told him she thought when he pulled her hair out, that he wanted it for himself, so she handed him the sack of her hair. After a very heated argument, he went back to the business and slept that night on the sofa in his office. (This story came from the beauty shop, where one of the clients heard it from Selena, then told it on the party line.)

It rained all that night and there were several large mud puddles in front of TJ's business. After TJ left following their argument, Selena took all of his tailor-made suits, monogrammed shirts, expensive Italian-made shoes, ties, hats and gold cuff links and put them in her car. Early next morning, she drove to his business with all the clothes she had picked out. She dumped them in the mud puddles, running over them with the car repeatedly before she left. She then packed all her things and moved out. All of this transpired before TJ woke up from his drunken night. He got into his car to go home when he saw his whole closet of clothes lying in the mud. He had intended to apologize to her. When he discovered what she had done with his clothes, he was furious! When he got home, everything that belonged to her was gone. All the years of their marriage had been, in a word, torrid. This incident made him realize that he really was about to lose her for good.

Selena's leaving was what brought TJ to religion. He asked a local popular preacher to come see him. When the preacher arrived, he asked him to help him pray to get Selena back, plus help him give up drinking. For this one-on-one assistance, he gave a large donation to the preacher's church. He then became close friends with this preacher, and for several months everyone thought he had made a change for the better.

The next spring, however, TJ was bored and Selena had not come back, so he purchased a very expensive small yacht for entertainment. For his boat's "christening," he invited the preacher and two old bar friends to go with him to a local lake to fish. They loaded up all their gear, including a shotgun that he had purchased and never used. Once away from shore, the friends brought out liquor, and . . . TJ lost his religion. The preacher became upset with him when he started drinking. They were in the middle of the lake when his drunkenness caused the preacher to berate him about the wicked ways of liquor, and the "road to hell." This made TJ mad! He went downstairs to the cabin and brought out the shotgun that he had bought when he was going to go duck hunting. He had never shot the gun and now aimed it while he was standing below on the stairs. No one was sure what he intended to shoot. He did not anticipate the recoil since he had never fired it. When he started firing, it knocked him backward into the cabin and blew a hole in the roof of the boat. He reloaded and aimed at the back of the boat and ended up shooting several more holes in the bottom. The boat started to sink. The two bar buddies jumped overboard and swam to shore as they feared he was getting ready to reload again.

Only TJ and the preacher remained on board. Some people said it was only the preacher praying that kept the boat afloat long enough for them to be rescued. This ended TJ's quest for heaven and desire to have Selena back. The preacher refused any other attempt to reform him.

The boat was hauled up next to the buildings housing the decoy ducks and sat there the rest of the time. It was never repaired or put in the water again. After the boat incident, TJ had dumped all of his drinking buddies except my daddy. Now Daddy seemed to be his best and only friend. They started riding around looking at crops and drinking every afternoon. When TJ got back to the business and parked the car, Daddy would attempt to walk home. On bad days they would just sit in his office and drink. This happened five days a week.

CHAPTER 40

MOTHER'S LITTLE ALIBI

When I was 9, I guess Mother had worn out her patience with Daddy and his drinking. There was a salesman, who came to our business and gave her the kind of attention she was not receiving from Daddy, as alcohol was still his love. She began to make excuses to go to a larger town to shop, go to the doctor, or take me to the movie. She had made arrangements to meet the salesman. She always took me with her then dropped me at one of the local movie theaters to see a movie the minute we came into the larger town.

When she took me with her the first time, I thought we were having an outing and I was excited because she had never gone to a movie with me. I was not sure what I was to do when I heard her explain to the movie manager that she could not take me to the doctor's office with her. She told him she wondered if it would be all right to leave me at the movie by myself. He was to make sure I did not leave with anyone but her. She then told him that she would give him some money to watch me and make sure I was safe. I was very upset about being left but was trying not to show it. She finally turned toward me to give me money for drinks and popcorn. She told me she would be back after the movie was over. I did not want to stay and I told her. She said I had to stay and I would be all right and she walked out the door.

As soon as she left, the manager told me to sit on an aisle seat so he could see me. I wanted to run out of the movie after Mother, but I did not see her anywhere. This town was large and I was afraid of getting lost. I sat down in the aisle seat and could not concentrate on the movie screen as I was surprised and hurt to have my mother leave me. After that, she repeated this at least twice a month, sometimes taking me out of school to go.

Movies ran continuously without a break and the lights were rarely turned on. The movie consisted of previews, cartoons and a feature film. Sometimes it also included a weekly serial or a "double feature" which meant two movies with two sets of cartoons. Many times, I would start watching it the second time before she would come to pick me up. I guess she thought taking me with her would keep Daddy from being suspicious of her many trips. This experience made me street smart for my age as I became suspicious of people and their intentions toward me.

However, the manager also had to handle collecting tickets, plus keep the projector going, so I was unattended most of the time. I always sat up close to the front of the theater on the end seat. In the afternoons, during the week, there were very few people watching the movie. In the summer it would be cold in the movies and I would pull the back of my dress over my shoulders to keep me warm, while I sat on my slip. Looking back, I am sure this innocent way of keeping warm received attention from any pedophiles in the audience.

I had noticed this man who started coming about the second week I was there. A few weeks later, I saw him again. He would get up to go to the lobby, and each time he came back in, he would move closer to me. He was an older man. The feature ended and most of the people had left. He finally approached me while I was sitting by myself then tried to put his arm around me and hold my hand. I was not sure what he wanted with me but I felt afraid so I jumped up and said "I need to go to the bathroom and I will be right back." Before he could react I ran up the aisle. I could not find the manager so I went into the girls' bathroom and stayed for a long time. Then I looked out for the man before I returned to my seat. If he was still there, I would tell the manager that I was afraid of that man. I saw the manager coming down from the projection room, ran to him and told him my story. He then seated me at the back where he could keep an eye on me. Before I sat down, I looked for the man and he had left. I told Mother and she said it was smart of me to do what I did and that she was proud of the manager's reaction. No more was said so I knew it would not help to continue the conversation.

There were two different movie theaters, and the other theater had a manager who took Mother's money but paid little attention to me. There was a different man who was hanging around this theater who was a lot younger than the one who appeared in the other theater. He was trying to offer me candy or money to come sit with him. I ignored him. He attempted to befriend me two times and then I never saw him again. I wondered if these men haunted these theaters every day. There were three different ones that I encountered in the two years I was dropped off. I was at the movie every other week and sometimes no one bothered me. As far as I know, neither manager ever told my mother if I had complained. She only had my word and I am not sure if she believed me.

I was only really frightened one time and it was at the second theater. There was a man who came in and sat across the aisle from me. I thought he was the man who had tried to give me candy once and asked me to sit down by him. I kept looking at him out of the corner of my eye and realized he was not that man. There were very few people in the theater that afternoon. I started up the aisle to go to the concession stand for popcorn and a Coke. As I turned into the aisle, he stepped out behind me then started following me, getting closer and closer. All of a sudden, he grabbed me by the wrist and started walking faster, pulling me along. I said loudly "Let go of me or I will scream." I kicked at him, losing my balance and falling forward. He nearly fell over me which caused him to lose his balance. As he tripped, I started screaming! The few people there all turned around and stared. When they did, he let go of me and rushed out the door. I picked myself up and ran to tell the manager who was standing in the lobby.

He said he was changing the film and did not notice anything going on, and that I should stay in my seat. I was mad, and scared as I thought he was accusing me of lying. I knew he heard me scream! I also knew he did not have time to come down the stairs and be standing in the lobby where I saw him. He was the one who was lying! Once again, I sat in the back row as close as possible to the bathroom until Mother came. While I waited, I noticed the manager kept looking at me, so I thought he knew I was not lying. He was trying to make up for his not paying attention to me, after Mother had paid him. I never saw this man in the movies again after that incident, but I was already nervous about going back there again.

When Mother picked me up, as we were walking out the door, I told her about the problem at the movies. I told her the man tried to take me out the door. She was very quiet. After I told her, I thought she would say, "I'm not going to leave you there anymore." Instead, she said "I'll just take you to the other movie or we'll check and see if he is there before I leave you." When I got in the car with her, she never asked about the movie or what the manager did. She would not look at me and I was near tears. After several miles, she said "It couldn't have been as bad as you said or the manager would have mentioned it. He said the man didn't hurt you." Then she said, "Don't tell Daddy what happened at the movies, he would be mad. Then you won't be able to go to the movies any more." I then realized that she had spoken to the manager and knew what had happened to me. She didn't believe me and she didn't care about me. I never did tell Daddy. My refusal to tell him had nothing to do with missing the movies. I didn't want to hurt him. It was hurtful to me that Mother was not concerned about me nor these men, even though I had been approached four times. I never spoke to her all the way home and I thought I would never forgive her.

Later, Mother became more brazen and would take me to dinner with her boyfriend after the movie. This cut the movie stay to a shorter time. I think she had begun to worry about these predators that I was dealing with each time. She explained that the boyfriend was just a friend, but not to tell my daddy because he had never liked this man. She said he would be upset. I knew a lot more than she thought. I had been to Sunday school and I knew what adultery was.

When we came home after these occasions, Daddy was already too drunk to care where we had been so I lived in my own little world of secrets, never finding a time I thought was appropriate to tell him. As I grew older, she would still leave for the distant towns, leaving Daddy and me home alone. If he was drinking, I had to take care of myself. When she would decide to have a longer time with her lover, she would go to a big city nearby supposedly for a doctor's appointment or shopping excursion and spend the night.

CHAPTER 41

ROSE

By this time, we had prospered enough that we had hired a housekeeper-cook named Rose who took care of me and lived in a two-room house on our farm. She was an older woman who had never been married but had been seeing a married man who came to visit her daily at 5:00 p.m. Her house sat by the dirt road, a county road that went between the city limits and our farm. Her job was to take care of me as well as the house. She would prepare our meals too. This also allowed me to stay home and not have to go to the movies anymore, since Rose could stay with me.

When Mother was gone overnight, I now had to stay with Rose in her small two-room house. One room of the house was a kitchen and the other room had a double bed and a small sofa. Mother was afraid to leave me with Daddy now that he was drunk daily. Mother could not take me and spend the night, so Rose was the answer. This interrupted Rose's lover's daily visit, which made her cranky. The farmhouse had no electricity or running water. She bathed in a tub for which she had to heat water. Her only entertainment was a radio powered by batteries with an antenna that ran up the side of the house. The antenna received the signal from local radio stations. I went to sleep many nights to the sound of Gospel music on her radio.

She had a small back porch where a large dog was chained up to protect her. Her only water source was a pitcher pump for water which sat out there. When I was thirsty, she would get a glass of water for me because I was not allowed on the back porch. "Bruiser" was a huge black-and-brown mutt who was her sole protection. This dog lived for the opportunity to bite you. The minute anyone attempted to step on the porch, Bruiser would pull the chain so tight you thought it would choke him to death, but it never did. Rose had an outhouse several steps from the porch. When I stayed with her, I had to go out the front door and around the house to reach the outhouse. I was always in fear that Bruiser's chain would break, because he was straining every muscle to get to me when he saw me in the backyard. If he got loose, I feared I would be eaten alive.

On one of Mother's out-of-town trips, Daddy became so drunk that he got in one of his "bob trucks" (which I think were three-quarter ton) and came down the dirt road to Rose's house. He honked repeatedly, while yelling for me to come to the door. When Rose came to the door instead, he told her he wanted to take me to the Dixie Queen for a milkshake. Rose said, "I can't let you take her, Mr. Lyle. Miss Ava would fire me if I did." My dad said, "I will fire you if you don't let me take her." She started crying so I told her it would be all right and I would come right back.

There were no seat belts in vehicles at this time. I was soon hanging on to the seat for dear life, as we bumped down the dirt road, swaying toward the left ditch and the right ditch. Daddy finally came to the highway to town. He pulled out in front of a car and nearly ran them off the road. When we reached our destination, he parked out by the road instead of pulling up in front. He opened the door and promptly fell out of the truck. He righted himself just enough to stagger up to the window to order the milkshakes. The Dixie Queen had only one window where they served their customers. There was no inside dining room. When Daddy approached the line, everyone moved away. He placed his order and dropped his money while trying to pay.

As usual, everyone was watching to see how this was going to turn out. He spilled half the milkshakes on himself as well as the pavement staggering back to the truck. We sat in silence and drank them. Every once in a while, he would smile at me and I would smile back. When we were finished, he asked me if I was ready to go home and we left the parking lot, barely missing two cars parked beside us. On the way back down the dirt road, he pulled over to throw up his milkshake. I guess liquor and milk products were not a good combination. He dropped me at Rose's house then drove on home. I could tell that Rose had been crying the whole time I was gone. She asked me not to tell my mother that she had let me go. I didn't need to tell anyone as several people in town saw us and someone was bound to tell. Additionally, our phone service was party line, and if only one person knew it they would call a friend, and even though the ring-tone number was to this one friend, several would pick up to listen. Soon the whole town would know.

Phone service was new to this rural community. The phone number assigned was whatever number was next when you had purchased your phone. Our business phone was three digits—221—but our home phone two years later was a four-digit. The phone company was located in a private home on a side street down town. When it was time for you to pay your bill, you knocked on the door. The operator, who handled all the phone calls, would put her headset down then let you in the door. If she received a call, she would stop your payment transaction and plug the small pegs into holes on the phone board to connect the two parties. If it was a business, you had a direct connection. If it was a private home, you would be on the "party line" and it would ring one, two, three or four times. If you were number one, you would answer. The other numbers were not supposed to pick up the phone. Nosy neighbors always did pick up. The operator-business office was gone in a couple of years but it was a unique experience to see the operator in action.

CHAPTER 42

HARVEST ACCIDENT

Three years later, the next required farm equipment trip came up in the fall. This was the busiest time of year for the parts department as it was harvest. Daddy attended alone as business had improved and Mother stayed home to take care of the farmer's parts needs. The only other employee there that day was the mechanic, Sherman, who was working on a tractor in the shop behind the parts department. What had started out as a normal fall day began to change as a weather front came through and the temperature began to drop dramatically, right after lunch. Sherman decided to close the garage doors as it had started to rain and the wind was blowing the rain and cold air into the shop. He must have forgotten about the fumes coming out the running tractor.

Mother, unaware that the back of the building had been closed up, sat down to work on some statements to be sent to customers. No farmers came in for parts as the rain had stopped the harvest. So, the front door remained closed. She began to feel sleepy but was struggling to stay awake when, at 3:30 p.m., Daddy and I came in the door. On the way home from the meeting, he had picked me up from school. The moment he stepped inside the door, he said, "My God, Ava open the doors!" Mother was sitting there motionless as though she was in a trance. The smell of the exhaust fumes was filling up the room and Daddy began to cough. He threw open both the front doors and ran back to the shop to open the back doors. I followed along.

The moment he walked into the shop, we saw Sherman lying in a puddle of oil on the floor, his tools beside him. The heavy gas fumes were like a cloud rising up in the shop. Daddy threw open the big overhead doors then dragged the mechanic outside into the rain. He sat him upright then pounded on his back. Herman began to cough and seemed to be recovering. Daddy then ran over to shut off the tractor. Next, he ran back to the front of the building to use the phone to call the ambulance for Sherman and take Mother outside. When Mother stood up to hand him the phone, she passed out, falling onto the concrete floor. Daddy called the local funeral home for the ambulance. All the while, he was trying to help Mother come to by hitting her on the back. I was standing in the front office coughing, totally worried and confused about what was happening.

Daddy turned around, then told me to go outside to stand in the rain. I just stood there in shock. He said "Go outside right now! You cannot stay in this building! They have carbon monoxide poisoning, which you and I will have too, if we don't get some fresh air." The ambulance was only five minutes away and they quickly loaded up Sherman, who seemed to be semiconscious. Mother was not conscious. Daddy had carried her to the car then left for the doctor's office in town which was inside the back of a local drug store. The doctor made a quick diagnosis then told him to take her immediately to the hospital which was twenty-four miles away. He said, "I don't know if she will make it." Daddy arrived there before the ambulance did even though they had left earlier. He completely forgot that I was standing in the rain in front of the business, with no coat and nowhere to go. I did know that I could not go back in the building because of the fumes. I had been left once again by my parents, to figure out my own way to get help.

Our old grocery store-home which was next door to the farm equipment business had been sold to an elderly couple who had opened a used furniture store where the grocery used to be. They were living in our old home. They had just moved in from another town about a week prior to this happening. I really did not know them. I had so many thoughts running through my head about this traumatic incident that I did not think of walking to our house in the rain. It was pouring down by this time and I was cold and confused.

I stepped upon the porch of our old home and knocked on their door. The tiniest little lady opened the door holding a big gray cat. When she saw me, she turned and left the door. I thought she was not going to let me in but she had gone for a towel to wrap around me. I said, "I'm Lydia and I used to live here." She told me to come on in and wrapped a quilt around the towel. I was shaking from the cold. When I had explained what was going on, she went in the back and came out with one of her dresses which she had me wear. She took my wet clothes and hung them on a rack next to the gas stove in the kitchen. The dress was almost a fit as she was not much bigger than me. She told me to sit down on the couch , cover up with the quilt and dry my hair with the towel. I did as she told me. Then it seemed like an eternity before I heard anything about my parents.

The police came looking for me, as once Daddy had Mother settled in the hospital, he remembered where he had left me. The police checked all around the farm equipment business and could not find me. Someone told them that Rose worked for us and took care of me. They went to Rose's house first, putting her in a state of panic because I was missing. She went with them to look for me because she knew who all my playmates were. The first place they started searching for me was our house, but it was locked up tight. They finally remembered that our old house had new occupants so they knocked on the door. By that time, I was dry and warm, drinking milk and eating cookies that the lady (who was called Tiny) had made for me. The cat had cuddled up to me so I was just fine. I was worried about where my parents were, but more concerned that my mother and Sherman were going to die. I was reassured by the police and Rose that they would be all right. However, both would have to stay in the hospital for a while. Mother and Sherman both experienced problems with their lungs later in life. Tiny and her husband became like grandparents to me after their wonderful kindness.

CHAPTER 43

GOOSE HUNTING

Another time, during the winter, Mother needed to take a city trip to the doctor, she said. I had been sick with a cold all week. Rose said she could not keep me as I would have to sleep with her, and she did not want to get sick. Mother decided to take a chance and allowed me to stay with Daddy. She left that evening and was to be back the following night. Very early the next morning, Daddy came into my bedroom and said, "Get up and get dressed, we're going goose hunting. Dress warm." I'd hunted with Daddy, but only squirrels and rabbits. I had no appropriate clothes for cold-weather hunting. I had on flannel pajamas so I put on my pants with a heavy long-sleeved shirt. I added a sweater plus my regular shoes and socks. When Daddy saw me, he said "You need a heavy coat, gloves and a hat." The only heavy coats I had were a Sunday dress coat or a school coat, that was really too small for me. The school coat won and when it was buttoned up, it was so tight because of the other layers I had on, I felt like I was tied up.

When his friend, Stan, honked the horn, we came outside to a hostile, unhappy hunter. "Where do you think *she's* going?" he said. My daddy explained the situation and Stan said, "I'll go hunting by myself before I have to drag along some kid!" Daddy said, "You do that, but you're not going hunting on my ground." He also added that I had been hunting before and I would not be any trouble. This sealed the deal that I was going or no one would.

I climbed in the truck and sat in the middle. The gearshift was in the floor, which left little room for my feet, especially after Stan put his coffee can, that he used for a spittoon for his tobacco juice, next to my leg. Every time the gearshift was engaged, it struck the coffee can and it sloshed the contents around. To further complicate the "juice can" dilemma, Stan's right hand was a hook due to a farming accident several years prior to this trip. With me in the way, he couldn't pull the can up close to his face to spit because the can was so slick with saliva that the metal hook wouldn't hold it. My solution was to cross my leg every time he needed to spit so he didn't spit on me. It was a long ride.

The destination was a goose pit dug in the ground on the farm. Nothing fancy, just a hole in the ground. We climbed down in and pulled a cover of camouflage over us made of trees and bushes. We settled in and waited for the sunrise. They both prepared their shotguns and waited. At that point, Daddy's daily drinking was beginning. He had brought along a flask of bourbon from which he took his first drink. He started to offer a drink to Stan when he noticed the tobacco ring around Stan's mouth. It was too late! Stan had seen the offered gesture and took the flask out of his hand. He took one long swig before handing it back. I thought if anything would have stopped Daddy's desire for another drink, that would have done it. I was wrong. A few minutes later, Daddy was using his sleeve to wipe the mouth of the bottle. Without any hesitation, he took another swig.

My feet were frozen. All I could think of was "Please Lord send the geese so they can get their limit, and we can go home." That prayer was answered as the sun came up followed shortly by the geese. The sunrise was beautiful and this was another unique experience that I would have loved had it not been so cold. Their shotguns soon leveled their limit. My ears were sore from the blasts. Earmuffs gave very little ear protection. I did not own a shotgun at the time so I did not have to shoot. My dad gave me a beautifully engraved Fox shotgun with a gold trigger a few years later on my birthday for duck hunting, but I never did use it to hunt geese.

After we went home, Daddy cleaned the geese between drinks, and I put on my warm socks to try and thaw my feet out. He thanked me for going so he didn't have to miss the hunt. I told him I had a good time but it wasn't quite the truth. If he had left Stan at home it would have been much more enjoyable and I would not smell like tobacco juice. He did not ask me not to tell Mother about him taking me hunting while I was sick, but I did not mention it to her. There was no one to tell her because no one saw us that morning, as there was no traffic between four and sunrise in the morning.

CHAPTER 44

PERILS OF FARMING

1953

There were always perils in farm equipment and farming. Many times, our business would experience some of the worst. The following is one that affected our family's business personally:

Daddy had sold a two-row corn picker to a close friend. The picker would be attached to the back of a tractor and was pulled across the field to pull the cornstalks down. A cast iron snapping roller would then strip the corn ear from the stalk, remove the husk, and place it in a cart that traveled behind the picker. Next, it would spit out the husk. Most of the time it worked, but sometimes, the husk or other debris would get hung up and stop the process. The farmer would get off the tractor and have to pull the clogged material out with his hand. You were supposed to turn off the picker when you did this. Being in a hurry to finish the harvest before bad weather would come, some people would not adhere to this simple safety practice. They would try to jerk the stoppage out by hand, but many times their strength was no competition for the pull of the snapping rollers.

I was playing in the shop with a farmer's son named Smitty that afternoon. His father was doing business at the parts counter. About that time, a truck pulled up with a corn picker on it. As they unloaded it at the shop door, Smitty and I ran to see what was being unloaded. There was some red liquid running down from the top of the rollers amidst the weeds and corn husk matter which was stuck in the picker.

Sherman, the mechanic, came out to converse with the driver and they both came to the spot where we were standing to talk about the clogging problem. We had lost interest and were about to leave until we heard the farmer say,

"They want the hand back as they want to bury it."

That comment glued us to the scene and Sherman noticed our curiosity and said,

"You two kids need to go up front and play."

I told Smitty to "follow me," for I knew a place we could hide and watch them. Daddy had built a set of steel racks that were stacked against the wall to hold large parts for repair. I had climbed up it before, trying to reach a bird's nest, and knew we would not be seen but we could see and hear them. At that moment Smitty's dad had finished his purchase and called Smitty to leave. He walked out the front door, and we waved goodbye. I squeezed between the racks and the wall to proceed up to my hiding place.

I heard Sherman say he could see the fingers but was not sure the hand was still whole. He asked how it happened and the farmer said the picker had stopped because it was clogged up with corn_husks and weeds. The farmhand had gotten off the tractor to pull out the stoppage and, even though he had been told to shut off the motor first, he did not. He must have thought because he had on heavy gloves, he could just pull on the matter without putting his hands too close to the working parts of the rollers.

He was pulling with both hands when the machine started

abruptly, running at full speed when the glove became caught up in the debris! He had managed to get off the other glove but was using his bare hand, trying to pull the other hand out of the glove. It was too late. The fingers were caught so it was impossible to stop the machine, as he had no way to get to the turnoff lever on the tractor. He was in the cornfield alone. When it got to his wrist, he had jerked his arm and the hand jammed up the machine again, but it was gone from his wrist. He was bleeding and screaming! One of the other workers was coming out to that area to bring some fresh water and heard him. He accelerated the truck, driving through the corn as a shortcut. It was the practice of the farm owner to always have first-aid supplies in the trucks with them. He jumped out of the truck and made a tourniquet on the farmhand's wrist to slow the bleeding. He immediately drove him to town for help. Fortunately, the doctor was able to save his life, but not his hand.

The farmer told Sherman he would be back later in the evening to pick up the machine and the hand. Sherman told him he should stay as he would do the job right now. Sherman knew if he left the picker with the hand there in the heat too long, the odor would be overpowering. He put on his gloves and a water-proof shop apron. The flies were already beginning to congregate on the bloody rollers as Sherman took the machine apart. He swatted them away and put his glasses on to get a better view. He struggled trying to pull the hand out. When he was finally able to get the hand released, he discovered it was terribly mangled. He reached back in and started looking through the debris for some of the fingers. He did find some, but others were shredded too small to matter. He placed them in a white paper sack that we used to carry machinery parts. The blood was already soaking through parts of the sack. He pulled out all the remaining debris from the rollers then washed the whole picker down, while looking for remaining pieces of flesh and bone. Now he was able to begin to reassemble it. Sherman took off his gloves and with the help of the farmer, loaded the picker back on the trailer. With a handshake and a thank you, the farmer backed out of the shop to take the picker and the hand back to the farm.

I was glad when it was over. I was sorry that I had seen this, but it was too late to come down without being caught. It made me sick at my stomach, and I could tell that Sherman was very upset as he picked up the bloody corn husks and weeds on the concrete drive. He put it all, including his gloves, in an incinerator to be set on fire. Next, he washed off all the blood and debris on the concrete. He then walked back into the shop to go back to work. I waited until no one was left outside then came down from my "perch." I never told my daddy what I had done until I was a grown woman.

CHAPTER 45

GIRLFRIENDS

When I was 10, girls finally moved into my neighborhood—two of them, named Virginia and Stella. I was very excited because I had met girls at school and wanted to play some of their games, plus learn other feminine things they did. I had found a best friend when I was 6 and had entered the first grade, named Edith. She had her hair in pigtails and I loved that. I asked my mother to braid my hair to look like Edith but that was not possible. My hair was so thick and curly that the braids were way too big to look pretty. I cried over it once and then gave up the idea. I played with Edith at school every day and we became life-time friends. When we weren't at school, I did not have any way to get to her house across town to play. She had a large family, so she didn't need someone to play with as much as I did. I would have liked to have had her over to spend the night, but our family problems with Daddy didn't allow that to happen. These new girls moving into our neighborhood gave me another option instead of just playing with the boys.

The new girls had moved into town in January. Virginia was from the city. Her family had moved into a building that was converted into a restaurant with housing in the back. It was directly across the street from our farm equipment business where I spent a lot of time after school. She was three years older than me but about the same size. She was not developed yet so we looked the same age. It was easy for me to walk across the street and play with her.

Her parents rarely let her cross the road to come to my house. Perhaps being from the city, they were not used to letting their child roam like I did. This did cut down on the adventures with the boys, but I enjoyed playing with her. Her parents were about my parents' age, but her mother looked considerably older. She was a very frail woman with extremely thin hair and you could see her scalp through it. She always appeared to be sleepy or just exhausted. Virginia's father always seemed to be in a hurry and was not particularly friendly.

Several months after they moved to town, Virginia and I were playing like we were circus performers. We were walking the length of the narrow wooden fence behind her home. We discovered milkweed pods on the vines on the side of the building. We picked them and climbed off the fence. Upon opening them, one by one, we threw the little seeds as high up as possible. They would separate into hundreds of little "helicopters" before spiraling to the ground. They would float on the breeze for a distance before landing. After a while, we had run out of pods and were becoming bored. On this particular day neither of us had a good idea for something else to do. We had tired of playing together so I was ready to leave.

Virginia did not want me to leave so she said, "Can you keep a secret?" Of course I said yes. Her parents were in their restaurant feeding their lunch crowd. She took me into her parents' bedroom, locked the door and crawled under the bed. She pulled out one of several cigar boxes and opened one. In it were syringes and white powder in little packages. Since we used a syringe to give my dad streptomycin for his TB treatment, I didn't find anything secretive about that. I had no clue what the white powder was. I decided it must be medicine for her mother, since she appeared to be sick. I said "Wow," and she seemed pleased, so we replaced the boxes. We snuck out the door unseen, and I went home for lunch.

About six months later, Virginia's parents were arrested for selling heroin. I had promised her I wouldn't tell about what she had showed me. I had never told anyone what I had seen under the bed. Now I knew what the white powder was. It was the first time I had ever heard of drugs, and the adults were talking about how her mother was "addicted." I was hanging on every word I heard when I was around the adults. They also arrested a large group in the black section of a nearby town. Virginia's dad had found someone there to help distribute the heroin. I had taken it all in, and now I had learned something new and bad. Her parents went to prison and she was sent back to the city to live with a relative. I kept my secret like I promised until now.

The other girl who moved in, lived across town from me. Her father had moved here to work for TJ's manufacturing company. Her name was Stella. She was a big-boned girl with blonde hair and freckles. She would sometimes ride to work with her father, then walk across the county road to play with me. She was the same age as me and in the same class at school. When we became acquainted, we started playing in the two barns located on our property. The little barn housed a horse named Sally, that I had been given by my parents. I had to walk a long distance from our house every day, carrying a bucket of water to her stall. I was in charge of feeding, grooming and exercising her.

Keeping the pigeons out of Sally's food was another responsibility that had been given to me. I had a pellet gun which I would take to the barn. I had started hunting with my father when I was 8. I was young but the same age he had been when he hunted for food on the island. The loft was a great place to shoot the pigeons who landed there. They would alight and work their way down to Sally's stall in order to try to eat her food. I would sit in the back corner of the barn and wait for the pigeons to land at the open door of the loft. I would then shoot them and throw them to the ground below the loft opening. After a few days of shooting, the pigeons would quit coming when they saw the carcasses of the dead birds.

I understand what people mean when they say "bird brain." Even though I had left the carcasses by the barn, it wouldn't be a week before the birds were back. I was a fair shot, as my dad had taught me how to safely use the gun. Since that time, I had been hunting with him and had improved quickly. The bird hunt in the barn had to be repeated more than once, so I was getting plenty of practice.

I always loved to climb in the little barn where Sally stayed. I could walk on the ledge above the stall doors until I came to a spot that was just the right size for me to climb into the loft. That way I didn't have to use the ladder that was built in. One day I was careless and missed the "spot" to step on, and fell back onto a fifty-gallon metal drum, breaking a bone in my left foot. I was not supposed to be climbing on anything that was not the ladder, so I didn't tell my parents. I walked around on the foot for two weeks with a limp and a lot of pain, however, I never told anyone what I had done. I had been told to climb the ladder in order to lay the rifle on the loft floor before I finished climbing up. Instead, I had it with me when I fell, and when it hit the side of the metal drum, it went off. The small hole caused by the pellet was not noticeable. If Daddy had found out, I would have lost the gun for being careless. I kept limping for almost two weeks. When Mother finally took me to the doctor, he said it had been broken, but it was too late to set it. He said I would probably experience problems with it when I got older. He was right.

Summer vacation before fifth grade had just started. Stella loved to ride Sally and we would take turns on her, or ride double at least three times a week. We would ride down the dirt road by the farm, to the far end, and visit Little Momma. She would give us a cookie while giving Sally an apple or a carrot. We'd turn Sally around and she would run back home a lot faster than she had when leaving the little barn. If you've ever had a horse, you would know that they are always in a bigger hurry to return than they are to leave their stall. Stella and I would then water and groom Sally, but Stella never volunteered to help clean out her stall.

One day when Stella came over, I said, "Let's go down to the big barn. There are several large, busted bales of hay on the ground. We can climb up in the loft and jump out into it." I was forbidden to jump out of the barn, but my parents were at work and it was Rose's day off. This looked like fun, and I thought no one would ever know. Right about that time, all three boys who were my constant buddies showed up. They wanted to jump also and suggested we play tag. We started running through the barn, climbing the ladder to the loft and running out the front door with a fast jump into the hay.

The third time we did this, I was in the lead to jump, landing in the hay. Stella was behind me but she jumped too quickly. Her right leg hit the back of my neck! It hurt terribly, but when I rolled out of the hay, Stella started screaming! When I looked back, her leg was broken and the bone was sticking out. The boys luckily had stopped in the door of the loft when they heard her scream. They came down the ladder quickly and I told them to go to my parents' business, which was close by, to tell them what happened. All three ran off together. I stayed with Stella, and it seemed it took forever for everyone to return. Stella was crying nonstop, which made me feel worse. My parents drove up the dirt road quickly, followed by Stella's mom and an ambulance from the local funeral home. Stella was loaded into the ambulance to be taken away.

After everyone left, neither Mother or Daddy said anything to me on the way back to the house. When we got inside, Mother said, "Go to your room." I can't tell you how long I was in my room or how badly my neck hurt. I was worried about my punishment, as I knew I had done a terrible thing, and I felt bad for Stella. I just knew that Mother was going to paddle me, so I was getting myself prepared. I knew if it was Daddy, it would not be a paddling, because he could punish me with a hard look and words. I could hear Mother and Daddy talking about what should be done to me, and about paying Stella's medical expenses.

After what seemed like forever, they came in and this is what they told me: "First, you are going to Stella's parents to apologize for causing this accident. We are not going to paddle you because that is too mild for this betrayal of our trust. As for Stella, you have ruined her summer. She can't go swimming, ride the horse, or play outside. The break is so severe that she may even be in traction. So, you are going to help her not be so confined. You will walk to the library every day, Monday through Friday, check out a book, walk to Stella's house and read the book to her. If she wants to play a game, you will play. Then you will walk back to the library, return that book and check out another for the next day. You can spend your summer missing out on fun since you have deprived her of her good times." I said okay.

Early the next morning they got me up to go to Stella's before her daddy went to work. Stella was still asleep and I can still remember the smell of the bacon frying in the kitchen. Her parents were surprised to see us! I told them how sorry I was and that it was my fault. They listened but did not respond. My mother then told them what my punishment was to be. They agreed that it was a good choice.

On the following day, I started this tedious punishment. At first, I think Stella enjoyed it, but eight weeks is a long time to endure this. She and I were bored with each other long before it was finished. The trip to the library was hard and I soon learned that I needed to pick out shorter books. Those were hard to find unless they were little kid's books. According to my parents, this was the worst punishment they could have given me. I soon agreed. A paddling would have been over in a few minutes and Stella would not have been on my mind in a few days. This kept her fresh on my mind and taught me to mind my parents. Stella's parents would not allow her to come play on the farm again. Before the first of the year, Stella's family moved away. No more girlfriends to play with.

After my experience with my broken foot, I did tell my parents about my neck. They took me to the doctor who said the area was swollen, but nothing was broken. The doctor told my parents that I was lucky it did not break my neck, as the blow Stella's leg took was very hard. I have never understood why I was not hurt more than I was. I guess the Lord had other plans for me. It took several weeks for me to get over the soreness but it was a good lesson.

CHAPTER 46

THE CANARY

Rose wanted to take me to a small city in another state which was only twenty-seven miles away. She wanted to visit her brother's family for the day, as well as to let them meet me. The real purpose of the trip was to bring home several items that she had stored in their garage. I was excited because we were going to ride a bus to our destination. I knew this was a special occasion because Mother insisted that I wear white. Mother had given enough money to Rose to buy our lunch in a nice restaurant. Early that morning the bus pulled into town, then we boarded and departed in a few minutes.

Once we arrived at the station, we walked to the downtown shopping district. I needed to go to the bathroom. Rose was shy and backward so would not ask for a bathroom. Her brother was not planning to pick us up until he finished work. Rose took me down an alley where she held up her jacket in front of me and told me to squat down to go. I did and then she said "Don't drink anything else today because we may not be able to find another place to go. Now hold up my jacket and stand in front of me while I go." I did as she asked, then we started walking through the downtown district looking in every store window.

During the walk, we came across a pet store. We looked at all the pets inside. I was playing with the puppies and admiring the fish. Rose kept looking at a canary in a cage in the back. She asked how much it was and the lady told her the amount. Rose looked at the money in her purse and said, "Let's go, I know you're tired of walking and you're hungry." We had already passed the restaurant for which Mother had given us lunch money. When we stepped outside the pet store, I said, "Rose, can we go in and eat there?" She replied "I'm not that hungry." She started walking toward a cart on the street that sold hot dogs and other sandwich items. She purchased two hot dogs and one drink. She then sat down on the curb. She took off her jacket, laid it on the curb and told me to sit down. I supposed she did not want me to get my white dress dirty. Later, I realized she did not want my parents to know she had fed me on the curb in order to keep their money.

We ate one hot dog each and I refused to share the drink. I reminded Rose that I had been told by my parents never to share food or drink. My tuberculosis in the past could be active again, and if someone else had the germ they could pass it to me. Also, not sharing would keep others from catching it from me, if my germ had been reactivated. She did not ask me what I wanted to drink. She got me a cup full of free water instead of buying another drink.

Shortly after our "lunch," her brother appeared with his wife. After introductions, we were taken to their house to visit and load up several things. These items were the things that belonged to Rose that they had been storing in their home. Their plan was to return us home, as there was no way to take all the items on the bus. There were boxes piled up between Rose's brother and his wife in the front seat. In the back seat were two cages containing six pullet hens and a rooster for Rose that was a gift from her brother. The cages were piled up on top of additional boxes. I was in the middle, next to the chickens, and Rose was on the outside with a hatbox and a purse in her lap. I didn't think I could be any more crowded in, but I was wrong.

Rose asked her brother to take her to the pet store. I stayed in the car while she went inside and purchased the canary along with the cage. She came back to the car then set the cage in my lap. After a few miles, the weight of the cage was hurting my legs, so she exchanged the hatbox for the cage. It was a hot, humid day and even with the windows down, the noise and smell of the chickens was overbearing. The rooster became agitated from the long ride and the restraint. He tried to peck me through the cage holes, so I had to use the hatbox to protect my leg and arm. When Rose's house was in sight, I was thankful to be back home.

I was never allowed to take another trip with Rose. Probably because I tattled to my parents about the lunch and the bird. I don't think my parents ever chastised her for using their money for herself. Mother said she thought Rose was just too "backward" to sit down in a restaurant. I thought she just wanted to use the money to buy the bird using my mother's lunch money she had given us.

CHAPTER 47

MOUNTAIN CLIMBERS

After the dangerous episode of injuring Stella while jumping out of the barn, Rose was told to monitor my play better.

I played on the farm in an out of the barns, climbed trees and engaged in various other dangerous activities, which kept Rose busy. The boys I used to play with had other friends who had moved nearby, so playtime with them was not as frequent since we had moved to the big house. The Monroy family in the small house behind TJ's business and across the street from our farm, were the only ones left to play with.

The Monroy family was composed of a widowed mother and five children—three boys and two girls. They attempted to live in this three-room house with one bathroom and one bedroom. When you walked in the front door, you saw a sofa and a double bed. There was a door to the bedroom which had a double bed and a twin bed. Mrs. Monroy was always busy cooking, cleaning and doing laundry. She washed all her clothes in the bathroom tub and hung them on a line out back to dry. The thing that stood out most in my mind was the kids only had one tooth-brush. She would put a pan of water on the stove and bring it to a boil. Each child would brush their teeth, then she would rinse the toothbrush, then dip it in the boiling water to prepare for the next child in line. They in turn would brush their teeth. The rinsing would be repeated until all had been brushed.

Mrs. Monroy had a brother who would come to spend the weekends. One of the boys would give up the bed for him to sleep. Martin, the boy who was my age, said they would take turns giving up their spot in bed to their uncle. I don't know what the uncle's source of income was, but he always brought food. There was no welfare or food stamps at that time, and his sister was dependent on him as well as the local churches' charity. We always had a large garden and we gave food to them during the summer. She canned these vegetables for her family. Other people helped with donations of food, too.

Directly across from their house were several catalpa trees in the fencerow on our farm. These trees would have beautiful white blooms in the spring and early summer. The trees were also home to catalpa worms, a type of black, green and yellow caterpillar which develops into a sphinx moth. The uncle and the boys would come over to our farm so that all the kids would climb the tree. We would pick the worms off the leaves and place them in a coffee can. This was not easy, because they were attached to the leaves they were eating. There was a sticky substance that got on your fingers when you picked them up. Sometimes they would cling onto your fingers as you were trying to hold the can with one hand and put them in with the other hand. Once you had a sufficient amount of worms, you were ready to fish.

The worms were then used for bait for catfish, bream and other species of fish. Fishing trips using this bait were always successful, as these large, bright-colored worms were a gourmet treat to the fish. The uncle would take the boys fishing with him. They would return with plenty of fish they had caught from a chute in the river. Their mother would prepare a big fried-fish dinner that evening. They always brought us some fish in gratitude for the worms. They would catch enough fish to feed their family for two or three days.

The largest catalpa tree had a big branch that went straight out. Martin and I decided we needed a tree house on that branch. We put a rope on a large wooden box we had found in the castoffs from TJ's dump pile. With both of us struggling with the rope, we pulled it up onto the limb. I got a hammer and nails from my daddy's workshop and we started nailing it to the branch and the main tree trunk. It was not level, but it was stuck in the tree good enough for us.

We played countless days in this box, being pirates, safari hunters, or cowboys and Indians. One day we decided to be mountain climbers. Then we decided it would be a good thing to tie the rope to a limb to walk up by putting our feet on the tree. We had seen this in a book. We tied a rope around our chest and, taking turns, we did this a couple of times, trying to see who could do it the fastest. On one of Martin's attempts, he did not tie the rope around his chest tight enough. He was almost to the top when he lost his grip and fell. During the fall, the rope slipped up around his neck and was choking him. He was trying to hold on to the rope above his neck but was panicking. I was scared he was going to choke to death! I had a knife in a scabbard which I was not supposed to play with, so I pulled it out and cut the small rope. He fell a long distance to the ground. I called his name and he did not answer. I thought he was dead! I rushed down the tree afraid of what I was going to find. But, when I got to his side, I discovered that the fall had only knocked the breath out of him. I told him not to tell anybody what had happened. The rope burns told on us when his mother saw his neck. She told my mother. I was in deep trouble because of the rope and the knife. I received another paddling and Rose received a lecture for not checking to see what I was doing with my time. Daddy cut the limb off that supported our tree house and burned it.

CHAPTER 48

MOTHER EXPOSED

The spring before I turned 11, Rose quit being our housekeeper and babysitter. She moved to another town. We never knew what the problem was but suspected that there was a breakup with her boyfriend. Maybe she wanted to get away from him and our town. She may have just wanted a less stressful job.

It must have been a year for breakups because Mother also found a new boyfriend. He lived in a town much closer than the one where she used to take me to the movies. She started wearing new jewelry that she said was costume that she had bought. She also received notes from him that she hid in one of her shoes. I was playing dress-up when I discovered the notes in the high heels I had put on. He mentioned the jewelry and said how beautiful she looked in it.

A few weeks later, I was on a school bus trip to another town when the bus had problems and the driver had to pull into a station halfway to our destination. As we were pulling in, a car was leaving, and my mother was in the front seat with her new beau. It took my breath away. She could see me and I could see her. I was so embarrassed! I thought I had kept it a secret, but now the whole town would know it. My mind said, *How dare she come this close to our home where she could be seen.* One of the boys said, "Lydia, I just saw your momma." I said in a mean tone of voice "No, you didn't." No one else said a word. The bus arrived back at the school before Mother came to pick me up. She was very late, but the bus driver and my teacher remained waiting with me. When she pulled up, I got in the car and did not speak to her the whole way home. She had nothing to say either. When we went in the house, Daddy was drunk and asleep in his chair. She covered him up and we went to bed.

The next morning at school, someone had written on the blackboard, "Lydia's momma is a whore." I was standing in the doorway of the classroom but the teacher had not come in the room yet. I was carrying a briefcase with books in it. All of the kids were looking at me to see what I would do. One of the other boys told me that Thomas had written it. He was the one who had mentioned Mother on the bus. I ran up to him because he was laughing! I gripped the briefcase with both hands and swung so hard that I knocked him out of his seat. I turned around and ran back to erase the blackboard before I started to my seat. Thomas picked himself up and started walking toward me. The teacher walked in at that moment and said, "Everybody in your seat." I glared at him and he glared back. He turned around and we both sat down. All the kids in the class were stunned, as I always tried to be a model student, but I had ruined that image. His face was red from where the briefcase had hit him. My face was red because I was mad. We both had time to cool down before recess. He never mentioned it again nor did anyone else. I don't know how Daddy could not have heard about it. If he did, he never said anything to me or my mother.

CHAPTER 49

BEEKEEPING

We still needed a new housekeeper to replace Rose. We tried one after another that Mother was not happy with. We finally found one named Jane who seemed to be working out all right, until the day Daddy decided to take up beekeeping for a hobby. About the same time, a stray dog which was a rat terrier mix, would come up to our house and start making himself at home. Soon he was a part of the family.

Daddy had ordered several hives of bees. The purpose was to help the pollination of the alfalfa. When they arrived at the local post office, we received a phone call from the postmaster saying we had to come right now and pick up the bees. I suppose no matter how hard they had tried to keep the bees contained, shipping by mail was not ideal. Small screen wire was the only thing holding the bees in, and one small punctured hole would allow them to start their escape. When I went with him to pick them up, only a few were in the lobby flying around. However, behind the post office boxes were several others and they were not happy, nor were the post office employees. Daddy had brought along some fine mesh cloth to plug any holes, but there was no way to get the ones that had escaped. I thought we needed a butterfly net, but the ceilings were high and it would probably have been useless. No one could reach high enough to catch them. We loaded all 6 boxes up to head for home. I don't how the employees handled the rest of the bees.

Daddy had already purchased the bee boxes along with the frames that hold the wax. The bees build the cells full of honey on these frames. He set up six bee boxes next to the wash house. Once the queen bee was put in these boxes, all the worker bees became very busy.

Jane, the new housekeeper, hated the bees milling all around the yard and out in the alfalfa fields. She could not understand that if you don't swat at them, they won't bother you. She had a habit of wearing some sweet floral perfume, and she always used too much. This attracted more bees to her. Daddy told her to leave off the perfume so that the bees would leave her alone, but she never did. You could hear her cussing under her breath when she carried clothes out of the wash house to the clothesline. Once she was standing still, as she was hanging the clothes on the line, the bees would begin to buzz around her. She would grab the next piece of laundry and start swinging at them. Occasionally she would get a sting. If she had stood still, as soon as the bees realized the perfume was not a flower they would probably have flown off, but she never could wait for that to happen.

One day, Daddy discovered that there was a nest of rats under the wash house. He hooked up a water hose and poured water into their entry hole. Once the water started pouring, one rat ran out of the hole. It ran toward the alfalfa field but not quickly enough to evade the rat terrier. The dog caught the rat by the head. As soon as the dog's jaw closed, he jerked the rat's head and broke his neck. He quickly lost interest in that rat, because a second one came out of the hole also and headed past him for the alfalfa field. The Rat Terrier seized the second one and broke his neck. Then out came the third rat, which instead of heading for the alfalfa, turned and ran through the bee boxes. The rat terrier took off at a dead run after him and caught the rat in the middle of the boxes. He snapped the head, broke the neck and when he turned to look back at the rat hole for another one, his back hip hit one of the boxes.

All the bees were aroused to protect their precious honey. They came flowing out of the bee boxes looking like a tornado. The dog, on high alert, started running as fast as he could around the house with the bees in pursuit. Daddy realized he would have to help the dog or they would kill him with all the multiple stings! He turned the faucet that was attached to the house on full blast and moved closer to the house so he could spray water on the dog as he completed the circle around the building. Not knowing that all this was going on, Jane stepped out into the breezeway to go get some eggs from the henhouse. The dog sped past her on the way around the house, nearly knocking her down. Some of the bees stopped to sting Jane, forgetting about the dog. The rest of the bees were hit by the water spray that Daddy was spraying on the dog. They gave up and went back to their hives. Whenever a bee stings you, it is only once. It pulls the stinger out of the bee. This causes instant death to the insect. Jane's stings were limited to just a few bees stinging her. She was only a few steps from where Daddy was with the water hose. We were grateful that more bees didn't sting her, because Daddy would have had to spray her, too.

Jane went in the house, told Mother that this was her last day, and she was going home. Mother couldn't worry about her right that moment, as the dog was so swollen from all of the bites that he looked like he was about to die. We went to the doctor's office because we did not have a vet. The doctor told us he could not treat the dog. We all looked so pitiful that the doctor said he would show us how to treat the dog. He gave us some medication and a syringe to use on him. Mother needed no instructions on how to employ the syringe as she had plenty of experience giving Daddy the tuberculosis injections. The doctor handed her the syringe with the medication. She gave the first shot of several she would have to give for him to survive. Soon after, Mother went to Jane's house and apologized. She volunteered to take her to the doctor. She said she only had ten stings, and her mother had put poultices on them. She also told my mother she didn't need our job, and she needed to find someone else to take her place. She told Mother that she had been warned about working for us. She said she had been told that I was hard to take care of and always into dangerous mischief. That she would have to manage an alcoholic, and his wife that was never home to take care of her family, if she took the job. She said you couldn't pay her enough money to continue staying there. Mother left without another word spoken and I could tell she was shaken up by this message. I thought I had found out what some people in the town really thought about us. But in my mind, I knew Jane was right.

It took three days of lying around the house, but the dog finally got better. We had never given the dog a name, and decided to change that right then. We decided on Pudgy, as he was so swollen, that seemed appropriate. He would never go to the wash house again. Pudgy was as smart as Jane. Mother was unable to find anyone else willing to do Jane's job, so she was my last babysitter and maid.

CHAPTER 50

MY LIFE ALMOST ENDS

It was my eleventh Christmas and Mother and Daddy's seventeenth year of marriage. All the drinking problems were beginning to come to a head. It was a few days before Christmas when Mother and I had gone to the city to finish shopping. This time I was not dropped off at the movies but indeed did go shopping. We were returning home about 9:00 p.m. and it had begun to sleet and spit snow. It was very dark in the driveway, and no lights were on in the house even though Dad's truck was in the garage. What we did not know is that Daddy and TJ had been on a drinking bout that had finished in a violent way. We never knew what caused the fight, but both were drunk. They had both threatened to kill each other. Each had an arsenal of guns that would have enabled them to do the job. TJ was never a hunter and was a terrible shot, but Daddy was a crack shot. Had Daddy not been drunk, I fear he would have killed TJ.

TJ's business was across the county road from our house. Daddy was in his bedroom on the west side of the house with all his guns and ammunition out. The door to his bedroom was open to the dining room. He and TJ had been shooting at each other across the road for more than forty-five minutes when we arrived. The local police were trying to get into TJ's building at that time and the state patrol had been called by the county sheriff to try and arrest Daddy. The county road between TJ and Daddy divided the town from the county, so someone besides the police was needed. Daddy was outside of city limits. All of these law-enforcement entities needed to be in position to resolve the problem for the arrest of both men involved.

Mother and I had driven in from the west and pulled in the garage at the time that the firing had ceased temporarily. We could not see the drama that was playing out on the other side of the house. We did not know at the time that the police were on the phone trying to talk TJ into giving himself up. TJ was preoccupied with his phone call so had quit shooting at our house. Daddy wasn't firing back because he wasn't being fired upon.

The house was dark when we stepped into the kitchen which led to the dining room. Mother had entered first and I was following her. We saw the silhouette of Daddy's body as the police had just turned their spotlight on the house. He had his back to us and heard the back door slam. He turned with his shotgun and fired! Mother had seen him turn and threw us both to the floor as the pellets sprayed across the dining-room table above us. He was such a good shot, that I have always believed that he was blinded by the spotlight, and, again, having too much to drink had likely helped, too.

Lying on the floor beneath the table, I could see the felt from the table cover falling in front of me. It looked like snow in the spotlight. The white tablecloth on top of the cover looked like a ghost costume with holes for the face as it waved in front of me in the breeze coming from the open window. Mother put her finger over her mouth as a signal to quiet me. She then motioned for me to follow her as we crawled from the dining room to the living room, and finally into the front bedroom. This seemed like an eternity. I could hear Daddy reloading the shotgun, and real- ized it was his double barrel. He was fumbling around trying to put in the shotgun shells but dropping them on the floor. It was a good time for us to get away but Mother did not know the gun was empty. He was standing in the dining room yelling obsceni- ties at TJ while he was looking at the back door. We were hiding between the wall and the bed in the front bedroom hoping he would not come to the front of the house. He walked into the living room and looked toward the front bedroom. I could feel my heart pounding in my head. I was wondering why Mother did not tell Daddy it was us. Later, I decided that she was afraid he was trying to kill us because he may have found out about her infidelity. We still were unaware of the "war" between TJ and Daddy.

Then TJ started firing at the house again. This caused Daddy to turn around and go back to the window in the back bedroom. This was the first time that we realized someone was shooting toward our house on the very side where we were hiding! Mother and I were waiting for a chance to crawl back to the living room and go out the window on the east side of the house. Hearing the repeated gunshots made us more aware that we were in danger not only from Daddy, but whoever was firing at the house. We had dropped our coats in the dining room when Daddy first fired his gun at us, and could not chance going back to get them as he would have a full view of that room. We could not crawl out the front bedroom window because, although Daddy would not be able to see us, whoever was firing on the house might shoot us. The east side was our only hope and Daddy had just left that space. We ran to the window and Mother pushed up the sash and she crawled out. She then helped me to the ground. Once out the window, we ran across our chat driveway and threw ourselves down into the hedges on the far side. From there we crawled until we came to the county ditch in front of our house.

About that time, Daddy remembered there had been someone in the house and returned to the back door. We had just started running along the ditch and there must have been enough light to see someone was running away. He still had not identified who we were. He fired the double barrel about the same time that Mother heard the door slam behind him! She grabbed me by my hair and pulled me into the ditch. The water in the ditch was cold and the temperature was barely above freezing. Ice, mud and water blew up all around us, soaking our clothes. The ditch was deep so I suppose he thought he had shot whoever it was, with them falling into the ditch. Regardless, he did not fire again. Our feet were wet and I had lost one of my shoes when I fell in.

Mother had been quite an athlete in high school and had never lost the ability to run. My legs were too short, and my stamina was not good due to my previous lung problems. She was dragging me and we both were crying. She kept saying, " Don't stop, we've got to get out of the range of that gun." We stayed in the ditch because it was deep enough he could not see us. I stepped on a piece of frozen ice and cut my foot, but we kept on running. We both were breathless. We saw a car coming and we jumped onto the highway. When they saw us, they started blinking their lights. It was my daddy's youngest brother, Amos. He said he had been driving up and down this stretch of road for over an hour. He had heard about the gunfight and knew we were coming home from shopping. He was hoping to stop us before we got to the house. We were relieved to see him. We were both wet, cold, frightened, and I was bleeding.

We stayed at my uncle's house across town that night while the law-enforcement people tried to find some way to subdue Daddy and TJ. The sheriff finally called an uncle, on my mother's side, who had been a deputy in the past. They asked him if he thought he could get Daddy to give up his guns. He said he would try. He yelled across the street, "This is Uncle Bob; would you let me come in just to talk to you?" After a period of arguing, Daddy decided to let him come in the house. Uncle Bob convinced him that he was going to be killed by the police or the state patrol, who were on the scene, if he did not come out with his hands up. He finally gave the shotgun to Uncle Bob, after he was told that TJ's guns were being confiscated, and he yelled to the officers to come on in. Meanwhile, the sheriff called Selena, the ex-wife that he had tried so hard to reconcile with, to talk TJ into giving his gun up. He was so happy to see her that it only took five minutes and he was convinced.

Daddy was handcuffed and taken to the county jail. TJ was taken to the city jail. Neither TJ nor Daddy would file charges against the other. They still had to stay in jail for a spell, but I don't know what the charges were at the time.

The authorities came to Mother and asked her to file charges against Daddy for attempted homicide but she didn't. They did not know that she and Amos, my dad's brother, had gone back to our house in the middle of the night to pick up all the guns, ammunition and casings they could find to remove all the evidence they thought might be harmful. The authorities thought Mother and Amos were going back to get clothes for the two of us because our other clothing was wet. One look at Mother made that story believable as she still was dressed in what she had on when we encountered Daddy. I was at uncle Amos' house in dry clothes and a bandaged foot, lying in bed. I was not asleep because I was worried about what was going to happen to my daddy. I finally fell asleep, but had terrible nightmares during the night.

Early the next day, Mother went back again then packed all of her clothes and mine to prepare us to move to another state. She said the purpose of moving out of state was because she did not want to testify if there were charges brought. Our Christmas was spent making this transition. She went to work for a bank, I entered a new school, and it was my first experience in an integrated school. We rented an apartment and Mother sued Daddy for a divorce.

We heard we'd made the news in our small town once again. I don't know what headlines the press used as I was in a state too far away to see them. I also wondered if TJ may have paid someone to not publish it, as he had done that in previous times when something went awry in his business. If it didn't make the press, I'm sure the party lines were "hot" for several days, keeping the phone operator busy.

When Daddy was released from jail, he wrote Mother and promised her that he would go to a hospital and get cured of the alcoholism. He was so shaken by the fact that he had nearly killed us both. I don't know if that fear or the divorce decree—or both —had helped him make this decision. He wrote Mother and me numerous letters from jail, telling us how much he loved us and how sorry he was about what he had done. He also continued writing from the cure facility. This was a very expensive program which lasted three months in a nearby city. He was a man of his word and took "the cure." It was successful! A month after he was released, we all moved back home.

Mother's lover continued to see her during this period of time and she had ample opportunity to get a divorce and marry him, if she had wanted. She did not. Instead, she told me that she was going to stay married to Daddy as long as I was living at home. Now, Aunt Ann had become my person to stay with while Mother continued her affair with her new lover. Aunt Ann was not aware that she was participating in this deception. The rest of the time when she left home for a tryst, she left me with Daddy.

I sometimes wondered if Mother's infidelity was due to Daddy's drinking or if Daddy's drinking was due to Mother's infidelity. A man that is drunk all the time is not a candidate for sex, and Mother was pretty and craved attention. After the cure was finished, I hoped that they would be different, but I suppose it was too late. She picked up a new lover, and Daddy continued to put up with it by pretending it was not happening. She must have loved him in her own strange way, and I know he never quit loving her. Regardless, they never divorced. She quit being unfaithful when she turned 55 years old. During their fifty-seventh year of marriage, she died.

We were the talk of the town for years, and all of the things Daddy had done caused him a lot of embarrassment now that he was sober. All the drama made him a recluse. He would not step foot in the small town. He had few friends and always entertained those he did have, at his home. He never traveled anywhere else except with family. He loved me dearly, and never spoke of the years of alcoholism he had experienced. I never brought it up. He was a good daddy when he was sober. When he was drunk, he had never been violent to either of us, until that Christmas. He died at 94 years of age after being sober for fifty-three years.

You may judge me and say it was a bad thing for me to tell this story about my own parents. They are dead and gone. In some ways, I would agree with you. My only hope is that other people who have had similar bad experiences in their lives will read it, and know that they are not the only ones harboring family secrets. I feel no hard feelings or hate for either of my parents for what I have experienced. I feel they both loved me in their own peculiar way. Mother just didn't know how to show it.

On her deathbed at 75 years of age, Mother told me that she was proud of me. She had never told me that before. Daddy was a much more affectionate parent with a lot of problems he couldn't resolve for a long time. I guess you could say I had a lot of "character building" in my life. I feel all of these events have added to my own outlook on life. Hopefully, it had a positive effect which helped me to be an open and caring person. I have always felt that the individual person is responsible for the way their life turns out. Spending a lifetime of blaming parents or others is a terrible waste. What bad things I have experienced I have tried not to replicate, but instead, to change for the good of my own family.

After the age of 11, I had to endure a lot of negative things as my life continued. Bad medical problems would follow me, as well as plenty of bad luck and drama within the family. But that's another story.

BIG MOMMA'S SAYINGS

***BIG MOMMA'S SAYINGS TO LIVE BY THAT I HAVE
USED SUCCESSFULLY; I HOPE THEY WILL HELP
YOU, TOO.***

The road to Hell is paved with good intentions!
(*Don't put off seeing a sick friend or giving a gift, a compliment or a
kind word to someone until it is too late*).

Give them their roses while they're living!
(*When you hear something flattering or complimentary about someone, tell them! They won't hear it if you save it for their eulogy*).

AND, MY FAVORITE
You will always love your children, but no one else will if you
don't make them mind!
(*You were not given this precious gift to be their friend. Your job is to
make them the kind of person who will be respected by all. This
respect is gained by their love and respect they show for others*).

TWO THINGS MY DADDY TAUGHT ME

Women are as smart as men and you can do anything you believe you can do.

Never back down from someone who threatens you. You will find most bullies are really cowards if you'll stand up to them.
(*I never forgot this and it has definitely influenced my life*).

Lydia

CHARACTERS

THE CLAYS
John and Callista Ryan Clay (Son Noble)
Noble and Clarissa Vaught Clay
Children: Alvin, Seth, James, John, Ann, Adeline, Ava Callista's
sister- in- law: Molly Albritton
Noble's half- sister: Tess Clay
Uncle Billy: Aunt Ann's husband
Eddie Baker: Ava's fiance
Uncle Bob-Favorite Uncle of Ava and Lyle

THE CONSTANTINES
Calvin and Maeve O'Brien Constantine
lnlaws: Tom and Ella Martin O'Brien
Children: Lola, Lyle, Matthew, Mason, Luke, Amos, Freda
Calvin's sister Susan Constantine
Grey: Calvins good friend

CHARACTERS IN STORY AFTER LYLE AND AVA MARRY.

Mable and Merl- grocery customers

Betty-child I threw off merry-go-round

Boy playmates-Robert, Chuckie, Will, Bobby

Sherman-Our mechanic

Business competitor-T.J. and Selena Denton

Rose and Jane-Maids and babysitters

Miss Beatrice-Piano Teacher

Mr. Morgan-Hog farmer

Marla-hospital companion

Miss Corbin-Pt grade teacher

Miss Tanner-Principal

Girlfriends-Edith, Virginia, Stella

Tiny-Elderly neighbor in our previous home

Smitty-friend at corn picker amputation

Henry: Honky-tonk pianist

ACKNOWLEDGMENTS

I would like to thank my husband of 57 years for the patience and love he has shown through the countless hours I have spent writing this book.

I would never have finished it without the help of my only daughter as well as my eldest son and his wife. They were the source of my technology help, that at my age, I so desperately needed. Their encouragement and love have kept me going.

A special thanks to Dan Petrosini, a Best Selling mystery author who was kind enough to offer me the inspiration I needed to bring it to the public as it was originally intended for my family only.

ABOUT THE AUTHOR

LYDIA CONSTANTINE

Lydia has always been very interested in Family History. Here, extended family have kept diaries, notebooks and merely paper accounts of the families that arrived her in the 1600's forward. These have been used for her sources until 1948 when she starts her own journey into her family story.

She is especially proud of her participation in the "Daughter's of the American Revolution." She has many patriots starting with the American Revolution followed by relative's participation in every war that has been fought through the Viet Nam War. She also has a relative that died at the Alamo.

She has a background in banking and served 23 years as the only woman on a Bank Board in her hometown. She also served as an Advisory Board Member for a National Diet Company plus owning 11 Diet Franchises throughout the Midwest and 2 Travel Agencies. Upon retiring, she accepted a job as Salesman for a new restaurant franchise which culminated in her acquiring the position of Administrative Director of the franchise. After retiring from that she spent every Tuesday with her grandchildren.

Always interested in community, as a young woman she was president of a women's Club receiving "Girl of the Year", Red Cross Chairman, winning the Southwestern Bell Award, Depot Museum President and Board Member introducing a new money raising campaign during her tenure.

She has 3 children, 5 grandchildren and 4 great grandchildren. She still plays Bridge, Golf, travels and gardens. This is the first book ever written and is a memoir under a Pen Name. The book was written for her family but she was encouraged to open it up to the public. She's not famous, but she has quite a story to tell. Tearful and funny moments. Her friends say:

"If something is going to happen, it will happen to her."